URBAN SHEPHERDS

Contact Information:

www.restorationacademy.org

TABLE OF CONTENTS

APPENDICES:

PREFACE

S omeone once joked that insanity is hereditary—you get it from your children. There have been times that my wife and I would probably have agreed, trying to raise four children far away from the support of grandparents. But, a greater truth is found in the words of Jesus that *"where your treasure is, there your heart will be also."* It was through the treasure of our children that my heart was first drawn to, and then captured by the work of God so evident at Restoration Academy.

As I've pondered the reality of the school celebrating its twentieth year of ministry, it dawned on me that I've been associated with this majestic and mysterious effort for half of its life. I've witnessed its continual transformation and maturation from a fledgling attempt to provide an environmental alternative for urban youth whose very surroundings were killing them, to a genuine educational vehicle breaking the chains of illiteracy and opening the doors of opportunity. I vividly recall the daily phone calls from my son, struggling to teach Antiquities and World Civilization, without textbooks, to roomfuls of urban youth unconvinced about the value of education itself, much less the lives of people forty centuries earlier. Nearly a decade later, Restoration students are taking AP courses and outscoring college freshmen in placement tests at local universities.

These are the types of stories legend are made of. But, the more beautiful story of Restoration Academy, that no amount of ink or photos can capture, is the inner transformation that is occurring regularly not only within the hearts and minds of students, but in all those whose lives intersect with this ministry. Suburban high school students driving 50 miles or more to tutor at RA find their own career choices being shaped by the names and faces of students they've met. Racial profiling—in both directions—is confronted with the reality of incarnational mercy and compassion as people of varying ethnicity and opportunity have to deal with the tangible fact of our shared humanity and common need of grace and forgiveness. Students' ideas of race are expanded as they watch the families of white faculty members buy homes in their own neighborhoods. The children of teachers are growing up truly "color-blind." People of means volunteering find themselves revisiting their values and lifestyles, not to mention their use of time and resources. I've watched leaders of major churches shrink their involvement elsewhere to increase their time on campus at Restoration Academy. For ten years I have witnessed the spiritual lives of people who have no common denominator aside from God's grace in Jesus, take root and sing in harmony in the "choir of ministry" that is Restoration Academy.

And all this is as it should be. God addresses "the poor" as a distinct people group, the objects of His biased favor. There is no category in Scripture for poverty as a social ill. God goes so far as to say through the prophet Isaiah, that to pour oneself out for the poor and needy is His preferred method of fasting, and the path to our own spiritual health. Jeremiah tells us without hesitation, that intimacy with God is evidenced by care for the poor. And Jesus tells us that our *kala erga*—our "beautiful deeds"—will cause others to recognize and honor God accurately. *Everyone* is a beneficiary in this ministry.

Restoration Academy is celebrating its twentieth birthday at a very significant moment in American history. I believe that two decades of sweat equity invested by a host too numerous to name, has set the table for a sweeter fellowship, unity, and labor for God's glory, manifested in the daily miracles happening in a tiny school in Fairfield, Alabama. This book, *Urban Shepherds*, will take you behind the veil to "holy ground." Walk slowly through its pages, and you will not walk away unchanged.

November 14, 2008
Fran Sciacca
Birmingham, Alabama

INTRODUCTION
by Ben Sciacca

"You will have the poor with you every day for the rest of your lives, but not me."

Jesus made this statement to His disciples when they angrily questioned the use of a poor woman's perfume. When they witnessed her pouring it out on Jesus they were indignant.

"That's criminal! This could have been sold for a lot and the money handed out to the poor," they said.

Jesus then informed them that the poor would always be with them, but that He would not be. He obviously was foreshadowing His own death, resurrection, and ascension. Yet his statement about the poor is often overlooked. He was indicating to the disciples that the poor were ubiquitous. They were inescapable. Poor and humble people could be found on every street corner. They would always be there. Yet, today in America, is that really the case?

How many poor people do we actually know by name? How many really poor people do we run into on a daily basis? There are poor people in America, but I'd wager that the majority of them are separated from us by miles and miles of interstate, by concrete and glass structures, and by the tinted glass of our automobiles. In America, we have the opportunity to physically separate ourselves from the lives of the poor. Sadly, many American Christians have done the same.

It is interesting that the narrative above (Matthew 26) directly follows one of Jesus most unsettling commentaries concerning the poor. In Matthew 25:31-46 Jesus informs us all that He will recognize us as His followers and ultimately separate His followers from the casual Christians by what they did or did not do for the poor, the hungry, and the naked. This passage jars me to the core every time I read it. He could have easily said He would recognize us by how regularly we went to church, by how faithfully we tithed, or by how kindly and lovingly we treated our family members, but He didn't. His criteria for faithfulness involved our love and compassion for what He called "the least of these." Yet, the most startling statement is He said that "to the extent that you did it to one of these brothers of Mine, even the least of them, you did it to Me" (vs. NASB). Jesus made it clear that our acts of compassion to the poor, hungry, and naked are actions unto Him.

The woman with the perfume took advantage of doing kindness to Christ while He was literally in her midst. However, the text in Matthew 25 indicates that we all still have an opportunity to lavish kindness upon Christ even though He is not physically in our presence by our acts of compassion to the poor and desolate in the world. This is amazing.

Yet, I fear that a good portion of the American church has either overlooked this passage or side-stepped it completely. We now know that 6,500 Africans will die by sundown because of AIDS, hunger, and treatable diseases. Nearly 4,000 babies will be murdered in the womb. Thousands of others will die around the world because of similar issues. On an international scale things are terrible in many parts of the world and yet a large portion of the church is doing next to nothing. Jesus commanded His disciples (those who would claim to be His followers) to aggressively do something about the suffering in the world. There is no "call" to such behavior. It is a clear command.

There is another haunting passage in Ezekiel 16 where God openly confronts His people and compares their sins to those of Sodom. In fact, He says Israel's sins were worse than those of Sodom. When most people hear the word "Sodom" they immediately think of the sexual perversions that Sodom was obviously guilty of in Genesis 19. Yet, in this passage in Ezekiel, God actually attacks Sodom for four sins besides their "abominations." God accused Sodom of having arrogance, abundant food, careless ease, and for not helping the poor and needy (v. 49). The Hebrew meaning for the word "help" actually means "to grasp the hand of." The inhabitants of Sodom refused to "grasp the hand" of the poor in the land. Grasping anyone's hand is an intimate and personal gesture. When we sit back for a moment and consider America (and the American Church for that matter) we have certainly been accused of being arrogant, and there is little doubt about the abundance of our food and the careless ease through which we live our lives, particularly when we compare ourselves to other parts of the world. Yet, when we get to the point of grasping the hands of the poor it becomes even more convicting. No one wants to be compared to Sodom, but any nation or group of people exhibiting the same sins shared in this passage can't help but be compared.

We are remiss to undermine or neglect the suffering going on around the world, but there is a world of suffering and neglect just miles down the road in most of our urban communities. In the small town of Fairfield, Alabama is a community that has been largely affected by drugs, violence, poor education, abuse and chaos. Close to seventy percent of the kids in the community are born into single-parent households. The same percent qualify for free or reduced lunches because they're living below the poverty line.

Restoration Academy is a lighthouse in Fairfield. The school that is now 20-years old. God started the academy through a man named Dr. Anthony Gordon as a response to the hopeless decay that was ravaging the urban communities in the Birmingham area (you can read more about his story in the interviews ahead). The school began as a rescue house to 69 high school boys. Most of them had been kicked out of public school. Today it is a school for children in grades K5 through 12th, and it is an institution of hope, learning, grace, and opportunity. With rigorous academic programs, top-notch instructors, cutting edge sports programs, and a biblically based curriculum and system of discipline, Restoration Academy is giving children in the Fairfield area a real chance at life.

If it weren't for Restoration Academy, what chance would Tarvaris Jones have? Tarvaris is sixteen years old, and his dad has been in prison since he was one. Tarvaris lives with his mom, and he's zoned for one of the roughest public schools in the Birmingham area. To describe Tarvaris as a phenomenal athlete would be an understatement. He's more than six feet tall, runs the 40-yard dash in 4.6 seconds, and already has drawn the attention of some NCAA Division football programs. Yet, Tarvaris is also testing post high school in math and reading, and he's only a junior. His reading comprehension is above grade-level. He's on pace to graduate as an A-B student with stellar test scores, a sound work ethic, and the life skills to make a bright future for himself. At the school he was zoned for, it's very possible that someone like Tarvaris would have become another statistic, another shining athlete that didn't quite make it. Now by God's good grace he probably will have the opportunity to go to college on a football scholarship, but he has the academic prowess to dominate in the classroom as well.

Another inspirational story surrounds Jerime and Steven Griffin. Both young men are orphans. They never met their dads and probably never will. They were adopted and they, along with their two younger brothers, attend the school. I can still recall the interview with Ms. Griffin (who adopted them) when she recounted with tears their desperate situation. She couldn't abandon these boys who had been abandoned by their father to a school system that would leave them high and dry as well. She came to Restoration Academy seeking hope for herself and the young men entrusted to her care. Jerime and Steven are excelling in the classroom and laying a foundation for themselves academically and spiritually. Their hope is that one day their own boys will grow up under their roof and under their authority, and that the legacy of abandonment will end.

These are just two snapshots, but their stories are telling. God gave Dr. Anthony Gordon a vision for the neglected, the poor, and the suffering and he responded. For more than twenty years Restoration Academy has been a vehicle whereby Matthew 25 could be lived out daily.

This book is about Restoration Academy. It's about the pioneers who God raised up to found the ministry. It's a book about the teachers in the trenches who have followed God's calling to lay down their lives. The book shares the testimonies of graduates who have gone on to do remarkable things with their lives. It exposes how God's heart beats for the lost and needy, and how He has used a small school for the last twenty years to help meet those needs.

Many believers sense an urge in their guts to get involved in ministry. The urge is no mystery, because it is the tug of the Holy Spirit as He calls all of us to get involved in what we were made for—to be agents of a holistic gospel to a suffering world. I hope this small book will help satisfy the urge for you the reader in many ways. I hope that you will be encouraged when you hear the stories. At the same time I hope you will be challenged to get involved either here at the school or in some form of ministry whether that is through funding, praying, or actually giving of yourself physically to get involved in the lives of others.

In Isaiah 58:5-12 God urges His people to engage the suffering and the hungry. The irony to His command here is that He promises to satisfy the hunger and needs of His own people once they begin satisfying the needs of those around them. Anyone who has truly plugged into a ministry that is close to God's heart will testify that they always emerge as the ultimate beneficiaries. In God's mysterious way, He ministers to us as we do ministry. We come most alive when we walk in His purposes for us. His chief purpose for us is to carry on the work of His Son Jesus Christ when He was on earth. Jesus explained His work in Luke 6:18:

"God's Spirit is upon me;
He's chosen me to preach the Message of good news
    to the poor,
Sent me to announce pardon to prisoners and
Recovery of sight to the blind,
To set the burdened and battered free,
To announce, 'This is God's year to act!'" (The
    Message translation)

For twenty years Restoration Academy has partnered with Christ in His dynamic work to bring hope, life, peace, and grace to the city.

The Apostle John wrote at the end of His gospel, "Now there were also many other things that Jesus did. Were every one of them to be written, I suppose that the world itself could not contain the books that would be written" (John 21:25 ESV). In similar fashion there is no way to document in one book all the stories and miracles that have taken place at Restoration Academy over the years. There was no way to interview all of the different teachers, office personnel, friends, and advocates who have championed this ministry for two decades. This humble project provides just a few brief but glorious snapshots of God's ongoing work through His people and His own miraculous hands.

CHAPTER 1

"That Was the Gospel" with Dr. Anthony Gordon and Bill Lewis

I sat there quietly for several hours as two great men shared their stories. Six of us were at a small round table tucked inside a cozy maroon room at the Fairhope Inn. Across from me sat the founder of our school, Dr. Anthony Gordon, one of the first African-American PCA ordained ministers. He planted a church in the Eastlake community in 1983. In faith, he started Restoration Academy in 1988 in response to a burden and calling from the Lord. As he sat there, his countenance reflected wisdom, a quiet peace and courage. To my left sat one of our school's greatest donors, Bill Lewis. Over the years, some at the school had come to call him "Our Angel." His generosity to our school had come like a divine rainstorm resuscitating our fragile ministry on several occasions. He was a venerable gentleman with white hair and a finely trimmed white goatee. His blue eyes sparkled with a unique light that revealed both life and joy.

Earlier that day, Paul Pankey one of our board members, Carl Lynn our Executive Director, Ty Williams our Development Director; and I drove south to Fairhope, Alabama to interview these two men who had been incredibly influential in the life of the school. As we unfolded the white linen napkins and placed them on our laps we small talked about life in Fairhope and reminisced about a few stories of days gone by. Shortly after, the waiter filled our cups with ice water, Carl brought us to the purpose of our gathering. For years different individuals advised us to capture the history of Restoration Academy. They relayed to us how visiting the school, hearing the stories, and witnessing God's hand at work had powerfully impacted their lives. They believed that this miraculous story should be in print so that countless others could witness the awesome story for themselves. To do such a story justice we determined that we would have to visit with and interview the man who initially responded to the vision God had given him, as well as the man God had used to help keep our school afloat during some critical moments. Every vision requires faith and effort, but it also requires the means to carry out that vision. For years God provided for the school, yet financially it truly limped along.

God in his own mysterious and marvelous ways provided a very unique subplot to the greater story surrounding these two gentlemen and our school. Who knew that just forty minutes outside of Mobile these two men's lives would nearly come full circle over lunch at the Fairhope Inn? Bill Lewis grew up in the white housing projects dubbed Birdville just outside the Brookley Air Force base near Mobile. Dr. Gordon grew up in the black housing projects in Pritchard. Both of these men grew up as perfect strangers within the circumference of the same city, and yet God brought them both back together to make a powerful impact in Birmingham. And so for nearly two hours we let these two men recount for us how and why they got involved at our school. Not wanting to miss a word I pulled a small digital recorder from my pocket and hit record.

CARL: **Talk a little bit about how you got involved at Restoration Academy after hearing about the school and its unique needs and challenges.**

BILL: After coming to Restoration Academy for the first time and seeing what was going on there, I could see that it was a hopeless situation. It was really peculiar because we went down to this beach house in Gulf Shores for the weekend and went to our little church down there. The sermon was on the way that the Lord loves the things that we can't do. And really His province is always the things that we can't do. Because if we can do it, you know, it's our job to do it. It's always God's province when we've reached the end of our tether, when we really can't do any more. And then I picked up a book, and then I think that our Bible reading—the same thing kept coming to me and I told Lorraine, "You know I'm being beaten up. The Lord is really talking to us." She said, "I agree and I think you need to reconsider." So by the time we got back to Birmingham I had done a complete about-face. I've forgotten whom I called; I called somebody and told them that we were going to be looking over our hand to see what we could do for the school.

That was really an interesting spiritual experience.

CARL: **What about your upbringings and your experiences would draw you to this type of mission? How did your background push you towards this type of mission or ministry?**

BILL: We were very, very poor and I empathize with people who are on the bottom end of the spectrum. This is what Restoration is doing. It isn't working for the 'haves.' It's working for the people the Lord calls "the least of these." I will always be a poor person; I mean psychologically I'm not capable of being a rich person. I was poor too long (laughs). But the idea of doing two things, one, helping some people in economically difficult circumstances and also helping them with what is sometimes as important as the economics and that is a spiritual structure. To some extent that is only partially true because a lot of those kids wouldn't even be in your school if there wasn't someone who cared about them spiritually.

DR. GORDON: In retrospect I look back on it I guess I can now see some of the underpinnings that inclined me to do it. But at the time I was just a young pastor trying to plant a church in the inner city, trying to do youth ministry, coming to the realization that that particular paradigm - trying to get with them on Thursdays or Wednesdays once a week for a couple of hours - I couldn't compete with the drug dealers; I couldn't compete with the street gangs. I started having to officiate or help officiate funerals for young African-American boys who had been literally murdered. After about the fifth one I sat down with one of my colleagues, Vernard Gant, and I said, 'We've got to start trying to raise these kids." So the school became a more practical vehicle to become their disciplers. I felt if we had them, the streets wouldn't have them. I wasn't an educator and didn't know the first thing about starting a school or running a school. I had heard that there were other small churches doing schools and went and observed them. I went and got some certification in Texas. We came back; we did the painting; we did the little carpentry. We did what we could; we put up signs. We said if anybody comes we'll have a school. The first day we had 69 kids at the door.

But in retrospect to hear your question, Mr. Lynn, I just felt over time that it was one of the best expressions of the gospel. I came up in a housing project. My father was murdered when I was five years old, and I saw my mother who was a very brilliant woman, in my mind anyway, get entangled in alcoholism and just lose almost all hope. And so instead of her being able to raise me I was basically trying to take care of her from about eight or nine years on growing up. There would be men in and out of the home and all the things that you might see. Now when I look back the beauty of it is I can remember my friend's neighbor who had nine kids and that lady, Mrs. Lafayette, telling me, "We're going to make room for you at this table, but if you ever steal anything I'll beat you half to death, but you can always eat here." **That was the gospel**. I don't know how she did it. I don't know how she fed her nine much less making room for me. I can remember another friend's father who I never saw him with a Bible. I never saw him be a quote-unquote godly man; in particular he wasn't a bad man. I can remember him coming across the street one day and saying to one of my mother's companions who had been physically hitting me. He said to him, "If you ever put your hand on him again I'll kill you." **To me that was the gospel** because this man had no concern to do that. I say all that to say that's what the school became about. We could have gone our own way each of us at this table. The gospel is going out into that ocean because somebody is drowning with the hope that God will bring us both back to shore, but with the risk that we both could drown. That is the heart of what the school became. And so it just became in time after time that same conclusion that Mr. Lewis came to year after year, my elders came to the same conclusion—we can't do this. Many times we tried to close the door. Many times we thought the door was closed and God kept it open until we could reach the bridge with guys like Ron Carter, yourself (Mr. Lynn), Mr. Williams, Sciacca, board members like Mr. Pankey, Mr. Longshore, sponsors, and friends like Mr. Lewis who could take the school to where it could be legitimate. Now it's a school that we can look at with great respect. At that time, the alternative was that kids were gonna die. GK Chesterton once said, "If something is worth doing it is even worth doing badly." And we did it badly until we could do it better.

CARL: **Talk about some of those challenges that could have shut the school down and some of the miracles you saw along the way in the lives of children, in the institution as a whole, how God provided supernaturally, obstacles, anything in there along the way.**

DR. GORDON: Just time after time ... I just don't see how we kept five, six, seven, eight teachers that easily could have left, because at times went two to three months where we didn't pay them. And we never had a teacher leave at mid term.

BILL: Now that's a miracle.

DR. GORDON: I was thinking about that this morning. We might have had some that said, "Hey,

Anthony, I've got a family" At the end of the term they said, "I've got to do what I've got to do." But we never had a teacher walk out. I just don't know how that happened over those years to have people, men and women, who had families and had a commitment to stay. So that's the biggest to me.

There were many other times when we couldn't pay our power bill. There would be five, six, seven hundred dollars. The power guy would come out to the school with the order to turn it off and he would look in the door and say, "I remember that kid; he was in a gang. What's he doing here?" He'd see his life turned around. He'd say, "I'll give you another week." And in another week we had the money.

Just time after time, where you know, parents would come in if they heard a rumor where we were going to close the school down and they would literally say, "This school saved my son's life; I want it to save my other son's life. Please, please keep it open." That touched the hearts of my leadership and they would say that we would have to give it another try.

BILL: I told my Bible study at my law firm about your teachers not walking off after being told that they were not going to be paid. I just said out loud, "I wonder how many of you guys would still be here if I announced that in one week that we weren't going to pay you." One of them said, "Please don't try." (laughs)

CARL: **I think that the testimony and the hopelessness of it is something that is outside your control and can't be controlled apart from God's intervention. It's so much bigger than all of us. That's certainly been a consistent theme. One-hundred percent of our seniors got accepted at college this year. Five of six are first generation college students.**

TY: **When you first brought this up to the congregation at your church, what did they say and think?**

DR. GORDON: Well they were…as one author has said, "there is a great lesson when you learn the difference between approval and support." They approved it, and you know the first day, who knew? Who knew what the real ramifications were? Well you know, it sounded okay. So there was no real opposition to crank it up. But once it got started there was always that tension and rightfully so to some degree. A young, small church again theoretically, rationally we shouldn't have been trying to do this. So they really had legitimate issues to raise. But at the same time I felt that as a church I never wanted us to be a monument or an institution. I wanted us to exist to do ministry. So I always said to them that, "We don't have to do outreach;

our greatest outreach is people coming to our door every day. Seventy-to-a-hundred families that come to us everyday. That is discipleship—it's right there." So I felt that it was in a good balance. Nobody ever really tried to just totally sabotage the efforts. But people objected and raised questions. And I think for the most part they were good questions to raise. But in the end the leadership in particular was always willing to say, "Hey, we just got to keep doing it until God makes it clear, until God makes it clear that He wants this school to shut down. And God can decide if and when He wants to. We gotta keep going on."

CARL: **What do you consider to be some of the key turning points, and that could be people being brought on board, things happening, moves, anything that comes to mind.**

DR. GORDON: Well, I think one of the first things was the football team. Mr. (Ron) Ingram, I believe was his name. He began to give us a lot of publicity (in the Birmingham News) and people just saw the name in the paper. Some people from Briarwood came initially out of that, and they would stay and help build a library, or help tutor, or help do other things. I think the notoriety that some of the sports were able to give us in the beginning led to other things that were much more important to the nature of the school, but the hook that brought them was the athletics.

I think we spoke already about the elders. I think the school's biggest turning point was when I stepped down as pastor and turned things over to one of my associates and reorganized the school independently. I approached Billy Longshore about incorporating and coming on the board, and that was the first time after about six or seven years that we even had some kind of stability or something beyond ourselves that could really even try to begin to stabilize. So that has led to obviously what we see with the board today.

Probably the biggest turning point in my mind is when Carl and Ron (Carter) came on. We spoke earlier about churches and leadership. One really unrealistic expectation that is put on leadership is to try to be the Michael Jordan ministry leader. There just aren't that many Michael Jordans. Very few leaders could do the kind of things excellently that need to be done. They need help; they need a team built around them, and when Ron and Carl came I began to have that team where I could accentuate my strengths and somebody else could cover my weaknesses.

When I knew from God that the school was going to really stand was when we reached the point where we started looking at this 66th Street Baptist

Church. It was a mile up from where I was. I would always drive up there and they would never say that they wanted to sell. One day I did my customary drive through and somebody was up there. The pastor actually was there and he said, "Well, we might be interested." He took it back to his deacons and they voted unanimously that they would be willing to sell. It had this big structure, a big playground and field, a big parking lot, and the whole thing. I said, "Okay this is it." They took it to their congregational vote and I think it went 95 percent opposition. That was one of the most crushing moments I had had in the history at Restoration. I was just so sure and then I found out where we were. We were about to move over into Woodlawn. The owners of the church at that point told us that at the end of the year that we were going to have to leave. So we had no place to go, no money, and then I get this call from this guy in Chicago, and he says, "We heard about the school." I think they had a nephew or somebody going to Christ Episcopal. He went up on a spring break and he talked about the school. He said, "Well we go around each year and we help build projects and we want to come to Birmingham and help you build your school." That was just more than coincidence.

CARL: **Do you remember the name of the group...? Mission Impossible.**

DR. GORDON: Mission Impossible (laughs). They came and took a donation that we had, $35,000 or whatever it was. That was the famous Milo's tea meeting where the construction guy told us just to order the first order of steel and it was going to be X amount of dollars, whatever it was, and that's all the money we had.

CARL: **In pledges...the contractor had no idea what that amount was.**

DR. GORDON: You know, as you say over and over again whenever it reached its lowest point God intervened and always brought some type of confirmation to say, "Are you through?" All I ever heard God keep saying to me was, "Anthony, are you through, are you through trying to come up with plan A, B and C? When you get through now I'll do what I need to do." So every time He would make sure that I was through, when I had exhausted everything that I knew to try and do, He would say, "Okay get out of the way. This was never yours to do in the first place, and I the Lord will sustain you." As He always said about Israel, "I'm going to do it in a way that when people see it they'll conclude it had to be God. When they see this they'll know Anthony wasn't smart enough, nobody else was big enough to do it and this school will still be standing. Even a pagan is gonna have to conclude there must be a God for this school to be standing."

CARL: **Well, I have a testimony to that. When we built the new gym and high school... and I can't tell you what that's done for the morale with them having their own place and athletics...our retention has grown a lot stronger. When we finished building it we approached three people about naming the building after them because we were told that's what you do. We approached you (pointed to Bill) and Billy Longshore, and someone else...I forget. Everyone said no. I realized that this isn't about men; it's about God and His glory. It's what you said, it's impossible. This was the first piece of architecture built on Gary Avenue in 50 years. You know, no one builds new buildings there...it's certainly to God's glory.**

BILL: Well, the notion that you were going to put my name on there after God did the work...(laughs)

CARL: **Well, we were told that's what you do. Tell me, Mr. Lewis, since your involvement what has God done through your life, your wife, your extended family. What's transpired since you started becoming involved with us?**

BILL: Transpired in what kind of way?

CARL: I mean how has God used it in the life of your family? When you talk about it what kinds of things do you say? What's going on in regards to that?

BILL: Part of everything that has happened to me from a spiritual standpoint simply reconfirms the spiritual truths that I was already learning in the Bible anyway, and learning in my Bible studies and Frank's (Barkers) teaching. We have obligations for the gifts that we've been given. You're given gifts and you're supposed to do something. You're not supposed to sit there...and then the great commandment to love your neighbor as yourself...what am I supposed to do? This project comes along and the question that you ask in your prayers is "Well, what do you do with this hopeless situation?" What is it that you actually do? Is it even presumptuous, okay, let's face it. What is Anthony doing? Here's the thing...here's the plan, here's the business plan. I'll present this to you since you're the business man (to Paul). What we're going to do is we're going to educate some people. They aren't going to pay for it and we're not going to pay for it. We're going to have buildings to build and we're going to have salaries to pay. How does this business plan sound now? Would you like to make a loan on this one?

PAUL PANKEY: The bank wouldn't have understood (laughs).

BILL: But you know the lesson that it has taught me is that in fact God does...if you plant and water God will honor your work by providing the increase, and you do have to plant and water. The point at which it becomes presumption is the problem. I think it gets back to being a part of the ultimate issue and that is—what was your heart like? What were you trying to do? I was a member of a church at one point and the church launched into and actually built a new sanctuary. If you look at the financial statements there wasn't any way to pay the debt, and somehow they managed to get a loan for it and how I'm not exactly certain. But they got a loan for building this sanctuary and the thing is that the old sanctuary was only partially full. I was thinking, you know, the spread between presumption and stepping out in faith is a little bit tricky but it has to do with the heart, okay? The truth is that the reason that God has stayed with this little school is because the original concept was not an ego strut. It was a heartfelt thing to do something that God was wanting to be done to begin with. The lessons that you had to learn with this thing—trying to do something that God wants you to do, and then if you plant and water, you're likely to see the increase. But if you do it simply for the purpose of making your-

self look good you very well just may get
yourself out on a huge limb. I think that's
the difference between a project like
Restoration which seems equally hopeless. Okay, in terms of the numbers it is
not any different from the new sanctuary.
But in terms of the motivating factors
I think there is all the difference in the
world.

CARL: **Doc, where you are now, are there any
faces of children, certain stories or lives
that stick with you?**

DR. GORDON: Yeah. Of course Michael Holley will
always have a place in my heart. Michael
was one of our first students in the high
school. He made it through the school.
He probably played in at least thirty football games and at least ninety basketball
games and I never saw a parent come to
a game, as was reflected of most of the
kids that we had. But I guess the moment
that touched me the most was the day he
brought his son to kindergarten. There
he was holding his son. Whether his son
stayed at Restoration or not I knew that
Michael was going to be a father there for
his son...a father that he had not had.

I guess on the other end of that one
of my most touching moments to me
was Omar Lee, a young man who had
a father, and his father helped carry our
equipment in the back of his truck when
we didn't have a bus. He was as a good

a father as you could find. I remember somebody interviewing him in an unofficial way, asking him, "Mr. Lee, what was the greatest experience you've had at Restoration?" He looked over at me and he said "That my son could have another father." He couldn't have a better father, not than the one that he had and for this man to say that he looked at me in that respect...

In one respect we did not have the environment and the infrastructure to prepare them to get to Annapolis. But there are young men who've made it. There are truck drivers and there are carpenters or they're doing something incredible with their lives. And, so that touches me often. So, it's story after story. In God's kingdom, just like they can't make it without us, we can't make it without them. We are not complete. We might have the money or the education or the diplomas. We can't make it home without what they have to give us. I couldn't rationally explain that to you because it would never make sense. It is never going to add up. What could they have to give? What could these kids or families give a successful man in real estate? But there is something that God has placed in them that seems unlikely, that seems improbable. But without them, that's the beauty of the kingdom, it's upside down. It doesn't make sense, but like David, he was trying to restore his family after the Amalekites had wiped them out. He was trying to get them. They find this Egyptian on the side of the road. He's just about to die. And David stops in the middle of trying to get his family, to get his wives and children; he stops and he bandages and restores this guy. And then the guy says, "Who are you looking for?" David says, "We are looking for our family, we're looking high and low for our families." The guy says, "I know where they are; I can take you to them." The most unlikely person, but that was exactly the person that David needed. In restoring him, he actually restored his family because that guy became the means. That's the overarching thing time and time again.

BILL: That's a great story. That's a great lesson. Every time I see somebody I think of when "You did it for the least of these you did it to me." In David's situation he goes because the Lord has told him to do that. The Lord says, "Okay this is what you get: Blessings." So that when I see somebody who needs help that sort of sticks in my mind. You know, is this an angel or is this the Lord actually? You know in some sense, anyway, it is the Lord. And all these children, all of these Restoration children are that way.

CARL: **Let me include a question. This will be my twelfth year at the school. You've been here, you've been away, you've** been back a little bit trying to catch up on where we are. Talk about how you've seen the ability of the school to holistically meet the needs of the children, even though it wasn't always that way. Talk about how you've seen that occur.

DR. GORDON: I just think God has brought people with the heart and the understanding of the vision that wasn't Anthony's. The vision isn't about trying to manufacture something; it's about revelation. It's just simply revealing what God has. I lost a lot of time in ministry trying to fax God an agenda, hoping that He would approve. And God said, "I don't need your agenda. I got one. Your job is just to communicate the one that I have. I don't need you, I have an agenda; you're just a vehicle to be used." So, as Mr. Lewis said when you start taking personalities and egos out then it's no longer about Ty, it's no longer about Carl, about Sciacca. It's about a vision that's been enduring and each one has been able to come to the table…and again the kingdom when you see it, you'll go back and I'm sure, Ty, the first time you got involved with Restoration you didn't think you'd end up being the Development Director. You came for something, but you saw the kingdom. You saw something that grabbed you in a way, and each of us could say the same thing. So I think that holistic thing has been that we've never been just a school trying to do a little ministry. At the core, we're a ministry that has the mission of being a school, and that's a big difference. It might sound like semantics. A lot of schools, Christian schools, they are the other way around. I've never had to convince that to anybody. They came with that, that's what grabbed them. Now, you have your style of leadership, your own way of doing things, but at the core of the vision, it's still the same. Now you've brought again the additional underpinnings and foundations to pursue that form of excellence where the academics and the responsibilities of being a school are now brought more to the forefront. At the same time it's the Coach Cokers. It's the heart of the matter that's there that has teachers buying into it, parents buying into it, board members buying into it. To me it just gets back to a vision that God has established, and we can just get out of the way and be conduits so that vision can allow people to see that people matter.

CARL: **Dr. Gordon we need to close by you sharing the story about the teacher that got you back in school. I don't want to put words in your mouth, but would you share that story?**

DR. GORDON: She had been my high school teacher. I had known her. I was actually a sophomore in college at the time. And I remember it had been a rough semester. I remember packing up to come home at Christmas and saying, "It can't get any worse than this." My sister knocked on the door and said, "Mom just died." I think I told a couple of friends. The first day school started back I didn't go back. I was 20 at that time, but this teacher had raised me through junior high and high school. I'm 20-years-old just sitting out in the park. This car skids up and this lady gets out and grabs me by the collar and says, "You're going back to school. You're either going to be dragged back or..." But that was the kind of character that was there. Our coaches, I can remember not playing a game because he knew I was an A student and I had a C average that week. It was that kind of path that we all had, that we took, and that we bring to the table and we translate it our own way, each of us, our life experiences we bring now to this mission.

CHAPTER 2

"Captaining the Titanic" with Carl Lynn

B IOGRAPHICAL SKETCH: *Carl Lynn started at Restoration Academy in 1996. He started his time at the school as a high school language arts, Bible, and history instructor. When Dr. Gordon stepped down as Executive Director, Ron Carter became the Executive Director, and Carl became the principal. Carl served as principal at the school for nearly three years until Ron Carter stepped down as Executive Director. He then took the reins and has been in that place ever since. Carl is married to Milly Lynn, and they live in Fairfield with their six children.*

BEN: Through this process of interviews, I've gotten a chance to talk to the different executive directors over the years, to Ron Carter and Dr. Anthony Gordon. You're the current executive director at the school, as you look back at the inception and where things are now, how have you really seen things change

43

in the progression over these twenty years?

CARL:

Well, as has been mentioned numerous times, it started as a salvage mission and what I guess stands out to me is it's always been something that is obviously a pure expression of the compassionate heart of God. Even with Dr. Gordon who just took in young men the first year. I used the analogy that it was much like mother Teresa in Calcutta who started a school by scratching the alphabet in the sand. She had nothing and eventually built schools there and all over the world. That's what Dr. Gordon did. He opened a dilapidated educational wing of a church, and took kids in and had a handful of people supporting him so it's such a wonderful part of the beginning of the school. It was a salvage mission, but what it has done over the years is it's increased its capacity to meet children at the point of their need and with holistic discipleship. And that story, as I've reflected on it, has been brought about because of God's people coming on board over the last decade and a half to two decades. It's really a story of His Church addressing the urban crisis. I think Restoration Academy really is a vehicle that allows the church to do what it's called to do, which is to address the urban crisis in this country. So it's really the story of God's people engaging in that ministry and I think about people like Billy Longshore who established the board. He was just a young guy, with not a lot of resources. He just heard the call and responded. And I think about people like Connie Edwards who came on board off the mission field in Africa and had a passion to develop a math program that could take students as far as they could go, including an AP calculus track. She's brought that about. I think about Barbara Barker, who to me really started our volunteer program, who just came and hung out until she figured it out. I've often times said she loitered until she figured out what she could do at the school in terms of her own calling ... Sonny Culp who's helped develop the board and take it to new levels ... Ty Williams who's had other job offers and could have done other things but has taken our development program to a new level ... Ben Sciacca who's brought an administrative excellence and also our distinctive of a culture of compassion, the school moving outside of its four walls. It really is a story of people who have come on board with their gifts and talents though they are inadequate to meet the need. God has multiplied it. He has grown and matured the school in such a way that kids are now holistically impacted because they are offering their gifts and talents. We are simply a trumpet to the church, that's what the school represents, saying "Come, join us as we address this urban crisis."

BEN: **When you first took the helm of the ship, I once heard you say you felt like you were the *captain of the Titanic* and you knew the end of the story. Flesh out a little bit of what you were experiencing at that point as you looked at the school and the ministry and then what's your vantage point as you look at things right now?**

CARL: I think that the greatest gift that the school gives to anybody is that it brings you to a place of utter dependency upon Christ. It stretches your faith. I've heard numerous people, board members, who say, "This is the thing that God has used in my life to increase my faith more than anything else." That's my testimony, too. Specifically, when I took the leadership, you just feel the pressure of this ministry. It's sustained by God's people and their willingness to give. And you just realize if that stopped, it would go away. There's no other means of support. We get a little bit from foundations and corporations and churches, but 90 percent is just from people who scholarship students and treat them like they are their own children - which is such a beautiful reality, but it's scary. It's scary to lead, and it's gotten stronger, but you know what, God will always keep us at a place where we are dependent upon him in this ministry. It should have, half-way though its history, it should have been shut down. If you looked at a balance sheet and saw the debt, and we were homeless... others have fleshed out this story... but it could have been just closed up. But it was because people of faith, like the Paul Pankeys and the Jimmy Mulvaneys and the Billy Longshores, the Alan Carters saying, "No, this thing needs to continue." Which is a miracle in and of itself that these men would take that step of faith to keep it afloat. That's just because they saw it as God's ministry. Even now where we are, we're looking at taking it further, maybe eventually duplicating the model across town, starting a boarding home, different things that continue to stretch our faiths. Even the fact that we're talking about expansion in the midst of a recession, you realize that people are men and women of faith who are involved in this school. I've often heard Sonny say that for our board, a great description would be that we're evangelical nobodies. We're not this board with a list of prominent, influential, affluential names. Yeah, we have some people that would fit that description, but mostly it's just people who are people of faith and they have sustained the ministry over the years just bringing what they have.

BEN:

I think Restoration Academy has been in Fairfield now for about ten or eleven years after relocating from Eastlake and you and Milly and your family were one of the first, if not the first, families to relocate into the community. You have shared passionately how you have a real heart for the ministry of incarnation of Christ becoming flesh and dwelling among us and have really championed that call for faculty and their families to move into the community. We've seen ten families, I believe, now occupy territory around the school. Why are you so passionate about that and why do you think that's a necessary ingredient to successful urban ministry?

CARL:

First of all it is the pattern of scripture. It's Jesus Emmanuel who became flesh and dwelt among us. I don't think that you can have substantive impact in ministry if there's not an incarnational element and the primary means of incarnation is the seven to nine hours that we get to have with kids every day. But it goes further and deeper when you get to live there 24 hours. I recently heard a stat that when a community has between 5 and 40 percent of what's called "high-status role models," that's business people, managers, educators, that community stays stable. But once it drops below 5 percent, teenage pregnancy and drop-out rates doubled.

When I read that, it encouraged me. Because we have just got to bump it up over the 5 percent. Just this past year two teachers moved in. It encourages me. These are people that mow their lawns, love their neighbors, call the police, take care of their community and that's what it takes. It doesn't take a massive amount of people. That's one of the beautiful lessons, and you read it in scripture, the fact that it takes a remnant. God whittled down Gideon's army from 10,000 to 300 so that He'd get the glory. It always just takes a few. That's encouraging.

I know that sociologists will give us real fancy definitions for what a stakeholder is - mine is very simple, it's when you fear that the gunshot that went off might hit your wife or children. At that point, you have no choice but to engage in the betterment of the community. It puts it on your front doorstep. If you stay the course, as you engage in the community, you begin to learn how to do it. But if you don't stay the course and you're not willing to overcome some discouragement, then you'll never see that reality and the fruit of your labor. I know that several of the people who have moved in have faced some difficulty, crime, houses being broken into, robbed at gunpoint ... things that don't often happen. I don't think that they're very routine but they do happen. You have to be willing to stick in there and then watch how God will use it to bless you. God has blessed my family through hardship that I've experienced at the school probably more than any other way. When you see God use what the enemy intended for evil for good, it really encourages you. But you kind of have to stay the course to do that, to see that.

BEN: **Let's pretend we can jump in a time machine to 2018. By God's grace, where do you see Restoration Academy and where do you see Fairfield particularly as it relates to Restoration Academy's key scripture of Isaiah 58:12 of "restoring streets of dwelling and rebuilding the ancient ruins." How do you see that by God's grace ten years from now?**

CARL: Well I don't think it's ever going to be a huge quantity. We always believe in quality over quantity so we'd rather go deep instead of just going out. So what that looks like in Fairfield is we'll probably have a school of 230-250 students, no more, because that discipleship model of an 18-to-1 student to teacher ratio is just absolutely essential in the mission. I do believe we will see more faculty and staff relocate. We always ask someone when they are hired, "Will you prayerfully consider it?" I don't believe that every faculty and staff person should live there but they should at least be pursuing that in prayer and then God will answer that accordingly.

I've said it before that I think we'll see some board members eventually relocate to communities like Fairfield. Parents, students, living around one another, being involved in one another's lives, impacting the community through its politics, through its housing, through its safety - just holistically impacting that community. We're tasting it right now, but I think we'll see it on a deeper level, and also I've mentioned a boarding home. We've got to develop opportunities to get some young people out of their living situations if we are going to reach them. For some we can reach them with seven-to-nine hours of discipleship. Others we need twenty-four hours of discipleship. We've done that kind of in an organic way through people like Coach Coker who have taken students in, but we want to be more intentional in our efforts, so I think we'll see that.

We might see the school model duplicated. We're praying about what it would look like in a community like Eastlake across town. Not that we always have to be the ones that duplicate. We could consult with others who are willing to do that. But we have learned through two decades of ministry, a lot from our mistakes, what to do and what not to do and those cultural distinctives that I believe won't change. They are non-negotiables. So I think we're going to be using that elsewhere. Whether or not we're doing it or we're helping others do it. I think that God will multiply it over time.

BEN: **Looking at the development side of things, what do you believe ultimately sustains not-for -profit ministries?**

CARL: I think the thing that sustains not-for - profit ministries is one word and that's "passion."

And that drives not-for -profits and really will decide whether or not they exist in the future and: 'Does your mission impassion the people that come in contact with it?' And I would say, "Without a doubt," because Restoration Academy will continue because it is a pure reflection of the compassionate heart of God. When you come in contact with it, through various means, but mostly by being on campus, seeing the students, seeing the ministry, seeing the community, it instills passion in you for the ministry and that ultimately is what sustains it. People talk about a lot of different things in development and fund raising strategies but chiefly "does your mission impassion the people that come in contact with it?"

CHAPTER 3

"One Step at a Time"
with Sonny Culp

BIOGRAPHICAL SKETCH: *Sonny Culp has been involved with Restoration Academy for five years. His first major involvement was following God's call to join the school as a board member. He helped play an instrumental role in the process of constructing the multi-purpose building which currently houses the ninth through 12th grades and the school gymnasium. After serving on the board for two years he followed God's call further and now serves the school as Chairman of the Board. He works for Graham and Company. He and wife Jenny along with their three children reside in Crestline.*

BEN:	**Sonny, there are several ministries here in town that you could be involved with. What is it about Restoration Academy that has drawn you in as a supporter and as a board member?**
SONNY:	Well, let me first say that what drew me in had to be my own heart. My heart had to

change and Restoration Academy is definitely a part of my testimony in that it has been the application of Ephesians 2:10 in my life. God brought me to the school years ago before I got really involved with it so I had some familiarity with it but I wasn't really plugged in. As I came closer to it, my heart really was not where it needed to be and thankfully God really changed my heart a few years ago.

The school was re-introduced to me and I started getting closer and closer. The thing that I would say to someone as an encouragement would be you don't have to be a seminary graduate to go help a ministry like Restoration Academy, but when you do approach it with a true heart for Christ then it will have a greater impact on you. Then you, in turn, can have a greater impact on it.

When people ask me, how I got involved with Restoration Academy, I tell them, it's truly **one step at a time** because as I said, I was introduced to the school well before I rededicated my life to Christ. But there was no fruit in my life particularly outwardly with helping other ministries. Sure I wrote a few checks every now and then, but I had no real relationship with any ministry. So of course what drew me to the school itself would be the authenticity of the ministry. I used to say as I would take guests out to the school, that knew nothing about the school, "You've now seen our secret weapon" so to speak and that would be the fact that so many of our teachers and staff have chosen to impact the community in which they live. They live there, they work there and they worship there by-and-large. So that has a real appeal, to see the gospel lived out. And if your heart is impacted already by Christ, you've surrendered your life, then when you see that, you're automatically drawn to it.

BEN: **What have you learned from some of these relationships you've had with the kids over the years?**

SONNY: I've learned that there are some great needs out there. I'm inadequate to fill all those needs, but I can do what I am called to do and that's the teaching of Matthew 25. To the extent, I can do that in an improving way, that's my real purpose in life. The kids are different, they come from different backgrounds and I have found that some of these kids, not all the kids come from desperate situations. But the ones who do have a very slim chance in life. They are going to end up in prison or dead and that breaks my heart.

BEN: **You've served as chairman of the board now for almost two years, when you look at the board at Restoration Academy what are some of the key qualities that you think identify the**

board when you think about them as a group?

SONNY: This is fun to talk about because about two years ago Carl brought to the attention of the board the book *Good to Great*. It's chapter 5, which talked about the "hedgehog principle. "And to Carl's credit, he identified 'What is it that Restoration Academy can be world class, or should attempt to be world class at?' Because as we all know, the needs are so great, we can't hit every need or attack every need. But what is it that we can be world class at, or should strive to be world class at? He asked the same question as it relates to the board... back to the school, the answer is the school can be world class in reading and math. We're trying to grow that into writing as well. But when you ask the question what can the board of this 501c3 be world class at? ... I would have never asked that question, to be honest with you, but Carl brought forth the opinion that we can be world class in two things... first of all in bringing guests out to the school on a consistent basis. We do a guest luncheon every month. We do not do golf tournaments and banquets as an intentional part of our fundraising, and yet we've seen our support base grow significantly over the last two years since we've implemented this strategy. Our board which is now up to fifteen, has generally been around ten to twelve, is very faithful about bringing guests out to this monthly luncheon and we find that our guests are bringing guests. Their hearts are impacted and some of them come and volunteer and some of them give money. So I would say our board is now world class in terms of doing this. We are having fifty to sixty people consistently at these monthly luncheons which three years ago, we would be thrilled to have up to fifteen people including board members. The second thing that we do is we want to be world class at saying 'thank you' to the people who give us money. We are very intentional about this.

BEN: **Are there any specific stories, students, events that have taken place in your time at the school that you think will stick with you for a long time?**

SONNY: Well there are many frankly... some of them funny... but there's one that goes back to a couple of years ago when we were just initiating the *Good to Great* strategy that we started. I had a phone call from one of my wife's friends named, Marcie. Marcie called me... she had known Jenny from at least 12 years prior through the Junior League of Birmingham. Marcie kept seeing my name in some of the industrial parks around Birmingham through my job, and she knew that I could help her get some leads as she now worked for Alabama Adventure

Amusement Park. So she showed up on the day of the appointment and she had a young African-American girl with her and she introduced me. Towards the end of our conversation I turned to Marcie and I said, "Now let me ask if you can help me. I'm on the board of a school in Fairfield and we have some great students that could be super employees for Alabama Adventure." Before I completed the sentence, the young girl, Toni, perked up with a big smile and said, "Do you mean Restoration Academy?" I said, "I certainly do." She said, "I graduated from there." It turns out she had gone on to the University of Alabama. She came to the school before the campus moved to Fairfield, really when the school, as you've read in this book, was very much a rescue mission. And the fact that she had graduated from the University of Alabama, probably one of the few graduates that we would have had in that era of the school was almost like an angel showing up in my office that day. When I got back to my desk that day, after the meeting, it really hit me that what are the odds that a four-year college graduate from Restoration Academy would show up in my office on a professional basis. I mean we have had graduating classes not too long ago of five and less and so what are the odds of that? I just knew God was telling me, or affirming for me, this is what you need to continue to do, is to advocate for Restoration Academy. That story will stick with me for a very long time.

BEN: **Your wife Jenny and some of your kids have gotten involved in the school as well. How have you seen the school really impact your family and affect them?**

SONNY: I'm very thankful that they've come on board with it. I will tell you, it has given my family something that we all need to have, a cause greater than ourselves. It doesn't have to be Restoration Academy, but it needs to be something. My wife volunteers in tutoring and she's very faithful about bringing guests out to the school consistently. We work together about who we're going to bring in terms of couples, perhaps one at a time. My children are very much aware. Another story that will stick with me for a long time was when I took my eight-year old son out to the school for a basketball game. When we arrived, I stopped and talked to a couple of teachers and some other people associated with the school. As we got to our seats, my son William, looked at me and said, "Dad how long have you worked at Restoration Academy?" And that was just the greatest reward of a comment that I could ever get from him.

BEN: **A lot has been said about the school's "hedgehog." From the vantage point of the Chairman could you elaborate?**

SONNY: We changed the profile of who our board member is. Our board member is very young on average. The last four or five board members that we have with the exception of one are all probably thirty-two and younger. So what we have found as we've gone forward with this new direction, this hedgehog, is that people are calling us to want to be on our board. And the captains of industry are not going to call you to ask to be on your board, they're busy… understandably so. But people who have a heart for what we talked about in this book, they *do* want to be involved and they *will* come to the luncheon every month and bring guests every month. And they *will* write the thank you notes. That's who we have as a board member. As I've said earlier - "a bunch of evangelical nobodies." We are, in football vernacular, the Little Sisters of the Poor in terms of boards. Most people I know of influence can look at our board and not know very many of them at all and I think that's the plan that God has given us, and we are executing that plan and God is definitely blessing it.

CHAPTER 4

"Holding the Arms of Moses" with Billy Longshore III and Bobby Nix

B IOGRAPHICAL SKETCH: *Billy Longshore has been actively involved with Restoration Academy longer than anyone. He incorporated the school as a non-profit corporation in 1995 when it was known as Frontier Christian School. He joined the advisory board in 1996 and finally helped formulate the working board in 1997. He served as Chairman of the school for nearly a decade. He has worked for years as an attorney at Longshore Buck & Longshore. He and his wife and his son reside in Indian Springs.*

Bobby Nix has been a close friend and supporter of the school for nearly twenty years. He served on the original advisory board and working board in the mid to late 1990s. He is the founder of The Right Stuff Ministries, which is an urban basketball ministry, and he currently serves as Executive Director of the Christian Service Mission. He and his wife and children reside in Leeds.

CARL: **Let's talk about how you were introduced to the school and what was your original reaction when you first came?**

BILLY: I met Anthony back in '84 to '87. Johnny Wilson was the Urban Young Life Director, and he had been the suburban area director and felt led to start an urban Young Life. I got involved in that as did Jimmy Mulvaney, Chip Bivens and those people, but Johnny met Anthony and got to be friends with him. This was about the time that Anthony had started his church. Anthony helped us out and went on a couple of camps with us, took off a week, and helped be a counselor in several places. That's how I got to know him. Then, I really kind of lost contact with him. Every now and then I'd run across him - until he called me. It was in late '95. He had a school going at the church, Frontier Christian School, and he wanted me to change the name to Restoration Academy and be its own entity, because they were going to merge with a church. They were kind of having several people coming together to go with this other church. As it turns out this church didn't merge in, they became a new entity. So Anthony came to me and told me what he was doing, and I didn't even know he had started a school. So I did the incorporation papers for Restoration Academy and went out to the school to see it at the church facility and was just amazed with all the kids out there. And I said, "How in the world are you running this thing?" And he said, "Through a lot of prayer." Then he asked if I would be on the advisory board, and we started having advisory board meetings at my office. Was that your first involvement, Bobby?

BOBBY: No, I was a little bit involved before then.

CARL: **I want to interject something that you have shared before, about the phone call from Clark Durant.**

BILLY: I was already involved a little on the advisory board, but anyway we started meeting in my office about once a month. It was Alan and Sally Carter, Terry and Pattie Gensemer, Bobby, "A.J." Arthur Johnson, and Anthony and Sharon (Gordon). The school became its own entity because it was going to move to a new church and split off from the old one. The next thing I really remember is—I went to graduation that May, and there was like twenty to twenty-three kids. I thought, man, it was really an inspiring graduation ceremony, and the place was packed. After the service I was just standing there talking to some people and somebody tapped me on the shoulder. I turned around and it was Arlene Cage. She would come once a week and clean my grandmother's house and clean my mom's house. She was putting her grandson through there because he had had some problems at the public schools, and he had straightened up and ended up going into the military. I thought, man, Arlene she was paying like $75 a month or more to get her grandson in, and I thought, man, that's a sacrifice for her.

And then the process of moving in that summer, I think I went there in late July and school was supposed to open in two weeks, and it was in shambles (laughs). Well, it wasn't ready. They were supposed to renovate and they didn't have the money. Anthony, of course, didn't tell me that they didn't have the money. I looked around and said, "Well, Anthony, how's the school going to be open?" He said, "Well, we need five thousand dollars, you know, to do all these things to pass inspection." So I wrote him a check for five thousand and he got going. I didn't even realize how desperate the school was. After one of those Hoboken Conferences, Clark Durant, who was, I guess, the chairman of the board of Cornerstone Christian School in Detroit, contacted me. They had like five or six hundred kids and had all these scholarship people, and he was the president or CEO of some big corporation up there, I don't know. He called me out of the blue. Apparently Anthony had been talking to him about needing some help, just pouring out his heart about all the struggles. Because Anthony, you know, a lot of times he would keep it all to himself. So Clark called me up and said, "You know Anthony is like Moses; his arms are weary and he can't hold them up any more. **He needs some people to come along side him and hold them up**. I think you need to take a leadership role in it." I was going, I don't know anything about a school, and I don't have any money, and I just got married and have a small child. I said, "I'll do what I can do." You know, he was talking about his board and all that stuff.

BOBBY: Yeah, we definitely didn't have a letter-head board.

BILLY: I said at best our board is single A or double A (laughs). I mean our advisory board, we're just people who care about what the school is doing, but we don't have any money or anything like that. So I kind of reluctantly said that I would see what I could do. We kept meeting, and trying. I don't know what kind of fund-raising efforts we took; we just started getting a few people out there every now and then.

BOBBY: It was very hodge-podge.

BILLY: Yeah, we were mainly there just to support to say "we're with you, we're praying for you." We'd go out there and we started some little thing like trying to get people to give to scholarship a student-kind of initial scholarship program. Sharon was kind of in charge of that, and it was just a few people that I knew like my dad and some other people would agree to do it. We'd have a meeting of the supporters, and it would be a very small group. (And I was trying to remember when the IRS thing happened...)

CARL: **I want Bobby to interject about his initial contact and reaction to the school.**

BOBBY: I probably got involved just a little bit before Billy did...really just out of developing a friendship with Anthony...similar to (Billy). I was on staff at Briarwood and the Lord had been leading me down this crazy, unlikely path of urban ministry, racial reconciliation and stuff. I got to know Anthony and we just clicked and he became one of my closest friends. That's how I got involved; it was really just out of caring for him. I didn't know doodlie about how to do a school or how to raise money or anything like that.

CARL: **What was your reaction to what you saw?**

BOBBY: On one hand I was very impressed. On the other hand I was like this is the most absurd thing I've ever seen. I mean, it was just in disarray. And I thought, "Well, am I imposing my own little WASPy (White Anglo Saxon Protestant) sensibilities towards this. And then I would argue with myself, "No, order is not a white thing," but then the other side of my brain would say, "Well at least he's doing it. Nobody else is doing it." But then I'd say, "It's just so haphazard." So I had this battle within myself, but the thing that held me in the center of it all was my love for Anthony. And then I got to know a lot of the kids and stuff. Cornerstone didn't exist then. Catholics were doing it, but I wasn't aware of an evangelical effort being made anywhere.

BILLY: I agree with Bobby, your first reaction is that this is unbelievable...

BOBBY: ...in a lot of different ways (laughing).

BILLY: Yeah, both good and bad. But he was like Moses. The children of Israel were a rabble rousing bunch, trying to get them all going in one direction and to quit complaining. I mean, he was Moses. He was trying to get them all to do right and line them up. He was everything from the fundraiser to the principal to the disciplinarian to the football coach to the bottle washer.

CARL: **Let's talk about key moments in the life of the school and how that affected your life personally.**

BILLY: We moved into the church facility in August and got it ready and approved by the skin of our teeth. I remember going out there and ya'll were having to run off the books. You didn't have books because you didn't know who was showing up. And who showed up was like a month long process during August. By September you figured out who was going to be there and you got the books ordered and it took another couple of weeks to get the books in. In the meanwhile the copy machine was getting run into the ground.

BOBBY: It was consuming like 30 percent of the budget to run copies (laughing).

BILLY: You had like two copies of the book until the new ones came in. Ya'll would have to photo copy all the lessons. You taught through photo copies for the first month of school. The school made it through that first year, and I met Ron Carter. Anthony and I had lunch with him downtown probably June or July of '97 and talked to him about being principal...

BOBBY: I was the first one to say something to him about it. We had taken a seminary class together and he was working in corporate and I just saw his heart. I just said, "You know what, I don't know if you've ever thought about this, but you'd make a great principal out at Restoration Academy."

BILLY: He became the principal in '97. He asked me about pay and I said, "Well, you and Anthony can agree about the salary but we hope that we can pay you every month." We were up front about it depending on what comes in. I was trying to remember the whole ordeal with the IRS...Anthony called me and said, "I need to come see you. The IRS agent has come out and has threatened to shut down the school because we owe back taxes." He confessed that he didn't have enough money to pay both the IRS and the teachers. We barely had enough to pay the teachers, so he was paying the teachers. I said, "Well how much do we owe?" He said he didn't know and the guy wasn't sure because they hadn't added it all up. So I called Catlin Cade and said, "Catlin we've got a problem; this school is a great school. We're in a mess." That's when Catlin volunteered his firm to take over our books. Nancy Wilson got involved then, because the books were just a mess.

BOBBY: He's an unsung hero.

BILLY: Yeah, Catlin, he's been a friend of mine for years. I said, "We don't really have any money to pay you. It would just be a labor of love if you can do it." He said, "Well,

I'll take a look at it." He did it for like four or five years, handling our books, or three or four years anyway, until we could take it back over. But about this same time, or shortly there after, we had this meeting. After talking with Anthony about this situation we decided that he needed help. We transitioned from an advisory board to a real board. We got Catlin involved, and shortly thereafter the pastor at our facility said that he'd give us until the spring of '99 to get out. He said that they wanted space for their own ministries. He and his group of elders or deacons were complaining that the kids were tearing up the place and that there was disorder and all this kind of stuff. They just didn't really want to be involved with it anymore. So we started looking around and we went to 66th Street Baptist. We met with the pastor and he was on board, and we met with the deacons—every one of them was on board. It's a Baptist church and you've got to bring it to the congregation and from what I could gather there were two or three older members who just said, "There is no way we want a bunch of black kids tearing up our church." I don't know if someone from the church we were using said something to them or what happened, but after that meeting the pastor called us back and said, "We're sorry, but we can't do it." It was about that time that Jim Pinto called...

CARL:	**You've got to back up just a little bit. There was a moment of decision on whether to lay the school down or whether to pick it up.**
BILLY:	It hadn't gotten to that yet. That's coming up. It's still in all of our minds. We weren't thinking that far ahead…
BOBBY:	If we could just move into 66th Street that was kind of going to get things back.
CARL:	**Did you know the total yet on the IRS?**
BILLY:	No. I told Anthony after we had that congregational meeting I thought it went pretty well. Out in the parking lot I remember it was in the spring time, or maybe February, it was cold. I told Anthony, "I know someone who has a stock gift, and they'd like to give it to the school. It will go toward renovations or wherever we have to move." Then 66th came back with the decision that they weren't going to do it. About that time Dave Upton was involved in helping us. He knew about our situation; somehow he went out to see Jim Pinto[1] at his church and it just clicked. It was probably March or April…
BOBBY:	That's not how it happened. It's going to sound like I'm tooting my own horn, but it's just factual. Anthony went on

vacation and while he was on vacation I was thinking about all this stuff. I just sat down at my computer, but I drew up some stair steps. Remember that? Well, I thought the way you solve a problem... when I was a kid I'd get these Highlight magazines and there was always a maze in the back. I'd always cheat. I'd start at the end and work my way back. I thought that's a good way for solving a problem, start at the end and work your way back. So that's what I started doing and I came up with a series of steps, and I was the one who told Mr. Upton about that piece of land in Fairfield.

BILLY: Oh, Jim Pinto's?

BOBBY: Yeah. I knew that that parking lot was just sitting there and the steps that I drew — if you'll get certain parties involved, and have like a master plan, put it on this site, get something worked out with the church, raise the money. It was a series of steps. So I drew it all up and it was like five or six pages, and when Anthony got back from vacation I called him and I said, "I want to show you something." I was scared to show it to him because I was afraid that he would think that I was trying to take over or run his business.

BILLY: That was before we went out to meet with Jim Pinto? Because I remember that meeting it was you and Jim...

BOBBY: Mama Louis.[2]

BILLY: Yeah, and me and Anthony.

BOBBY: We met in the green room of the sanctuary.

BILLY: I just remember that the meeting went extremely well.

BOBBY: When I showed it to Anthony, first of all, he wept. He said, "This is God." He was like overwhelmed. That made me feel better because I was apprehensive. Then it was funny; it was almost to a T...I wish everything in my life worked out like that. It was one of the few things that has. It clicked.

BILLY: It was like it was meant to be. God just showed it to everybody.

Bobby: And I guess I was naïve about it, not realizing, man, because if this happens it's going to be very difficult. I was naïve and inexperienced and didn't know that what I was setting forth was supposed to be hard. I'd probably be scared to death to do it now. I know too much now.

Billy: Then we met with them out there and Jim Pinto met with Kirby Sevier and some other people. They called and said, "If you build your school out here, we'll donate the church parking lot." And we looked at other places in Fairfield.

BOBBY: We looked at where the gym is now.

BILLY: And the Baptist church. I met the pastor through the Baptist circles. I called the guy who is in charge of the Baptist association. He called the pastor there. He introduced me to him. I talked to him. We had the same problem. They weren't really using their education wing; they didn't really want to let us use it. So we became concerned. It just seemed like, "Well, God, I guess you want us to build in this parking lot." The parking lot just didn't really seem that big when you looked at it. It just seemed like you were hemmed in.

BOBBY: Well, Mayor (Larry) Langford did a lot for us. There's no reason legally how we would ever build a building that close to a street. He moved telephone poles for us.

BILLY: You know you're not supposed to be able to build five feet from the sidewalk. They waived all of that for us. But we're getting ahead of ourselves there. The next big meeting we had was here in (Billy's law office). Maybe you had set it up through Roxanne's connections with some architect that was going to draw us a real basic plan, and he did. And we gave it to Don Pierson to price it out, and Don came back with a price that was going to be right at about a million dollars. About that time Catlin had figured out our tax liability, and I realized that my friend's gift to help give us a jump start on the building was about to cover the tax liability.

CARL: **You have to put the amount.**

BILLY: My friend's gift was going to be about $70,000. I was all pumped that it was going to go to this new building, and I had just this sickening stomach churning thing when Catlin told me how much we owed the IRS and I realized that this gift to the school was going to the IRS. I was going, "Oh Lord!" Like Paul (Pankey)... he would have had a stroke. It's like writing a check to the IRS (laughing).

BOBBY: There ain't nothing glamorous about that. There are one in a million people that would have done that.

BILLY: If we were going to move forward we had to do that. Anyway that came up about the same time as the building plan. It was absurd. Everything was just so absurd. It was going to cost a million dollars to build that building. We were behind on payroll. We owed the IRS seventy grand. And we were sitting around talking about building a million dollar building, and moving the school across to the other side of town. I remember when we heard the million dollar price, Jimmy (Mulvaney) was sitting probably sitting where you're sitting. Nobody said anything. It was just absolute silence when we were given the number, and there were probably seven or eight of us in here...Alan Carter and others. Finally Jimmy broke the silence and he goes, "Ya'll this is crazy" (laughs). He didn't say to shut down the school or anything. We started saying, "Well, for some reason God has brought us to this point. Maybe this is the Jordan River we're supposed to cross." But we still didn't know how to do it. We had no idea how do you raise a million dollars? How do you keep money coming in to pay the teachers?

BOBBY:

I remember thinking too — *are we trying to keep something alive that God is trying to shut down*? There were two clear choices here. We were either absolute fools or we were really, really, really faithful. We couldn't discern which one we were.

BILLY:

That board meeting was the one where we kind of were wrestling with that issue. It was probably in June or July. It was in the summertime. I think we kind of decided, "Well, we think that the Lord wants this school to exist. And we're going to take steps in that direction."

BOBBY: We just didn't have the guts to shut it down.

BILLY: Because every time you saw it in action, you were like, "This is of the Lord."

TY: **It seems like you guys were right there at the line. Was there anyone who kind spoke up?**

BILLY: That was just kind of the consensus. Everybody agreed from a human stand-point that this thing was toast. That was pretty unanimous.

BOBBY: Yeah, it was sort of like that movie with Robert Redford and Paul Newman. The one where they jump of the cliff and say, "Ohhhhh s_____." (lots of laughter).

CARL: **Oh, the cowboy one?**

BOBBY: Yeah, we all just decided to jump at the same time. It wasn't like there was a contrarian at the table.

BILLY: And we didn't really make the commit-ment to build the building then; that was later. We talked to Frank Barker and other people and he helped put together a lunch. We had a little meeting there. We had some business men and other people there, and we told them about our plans. That was our first fundraising effort and we got a few little gifts. Dave Upton was really helping and he was trying to stir the pot. We had other names, Peter Weston, and we would meet and we would talk about what we were going to do, strategizing about how we were going to raise money. We're still thinking, "There's no way." I mean, you'd wake up in the middle of the night going, "I don't know."

BOBBY: It was painful.

BILLY: Plus the time limit was running out. Here we are up in the fall of '98 and we have got to have a new school opened by August of '99. And you've got to have time for construction.

BOBBY: Did the school go straight from the church facility to the new building?

CARL: Yeah, we had one year to pull it off, or less than that.

BOBBY: That was when we had a meeting in November right before Thanksgiving on a Monday. Somebody from Jim Pinto's church had been up in Chicago and somehow got connected with this Mission Impossible group.

BILLY: Well yeah, they agreed to house the Mission Impossible team from Chicago. But when they came down we went out there and they had heard about us wanting to build the building. I came straight from the YMCA and so I was real thirsty, and they had Milo's tea. I downed about five Milo's tea glasses. That's where that story came from, and man, I was pumped…that caffeine and sugar. And I guess God used that to get me off the dime on the thing.

BOBBY: That became a running joke, the Milo's tea.

BILLY: Yeah. Dan Cassidy (from Mission Impossible) was there and maybe the principal for Aurora Christian School who was kind of in charge of it. They were there. They said, "This is just amazing what you guys are trying to do. We normally visit sites and then have a meeting and decide if we're going to do this project or not, or pick between them. But we feel like we want to commit right now. If ya'll commit to building this school we'll commit to bring a crew down."

BILLY: I said, "Well, you came to the right place." I thought, "Well God you have a sense of humor." So in combination with the Spirit prodding me and Milo's tea pumping me up I said, "We're going to do this, we're going to order the building." I said, "Don (Pearson), order the building. We're doing this thing." All we had was the $35,000 pledge from Briarwood. Don didn't know we had this pledge. I said to Don, "How much of a down payment do you need to order the building?" He

79

said, "Well it's two hundred or whatever thousand dollars, and I'd need about $35,000." That was the amount of the pledge. We were talking about the board having faith and all that. The person that really stepped out on a limb more than anybody was Don Pearson. Don Pearson ordered a $275,000 steel-framed building, knowing that we just gave him all the money we had. It wasn't our names on the line having to pay for that steel when it came in. It was Don Pearson. This is a humorous thing; do you remember you called me on your cell? You had gone to Briarwood and gotten the check.

BOBBY: Getting a hand-cut check for $35,000 out of Briarwood's accounting office in one day, it had to be the favor of God, because I had to run and meet Don at the Galleria.

BILLY: You were calling me on your cell phone driving from Briarwood to the Galleria. You said, "I got the check and I'm going to meet Don. Do you have any last minute reservations about what we're doing?" (Lots of laughter) Because he still hadn't ordered the building yet until we gave him the check. I said something like, "Bobby, I'm scared to death, but I think we're supposed to do this." You said, "Yeah, I think so too." We said, "We hope so."

BOBBY: It was like time was really of the essence.

BILLY: Don said we've got to get this thing cranking or we're not going to make it. So this was the end of November. Let me back up slightly from that because somebody else got involved with the school. This was his first involvement with the school. It was November 10th or something, and I was bringing a group of guys, including Brad Allison out from Altadena Valley, and there was a gentleman from Briarwood that was going to meet us there by the name of Paul Pankey.

BOBBY: Paul Pankey enters the scene (chuckles).

BILLY: That was November the 10th 1998. And so we toured the school, and it was a rainy, cold day in November. Brad Allison was just astounded with what was going on, and we went to eat at VeeJays on the Runway afterwards and they just couldn't believe it. He told me, "For the four Sundays in December we're going to take a love offering for Restoration Academy for what ya'll are trying to do." They ended up raising about $50,000 in cash in December from that small church. Then, Mr. Upton prevailed upon Steve and David Upton. They had just sold out their business, and they gave $200,000. Paul Wills, who was the older gentlemen that Dr. Gordon had become friends with and who was mentoring him some, pledged $125,000 over three years. But when he saw how desperate we were, he went ahead and gave it all in one year. We had the groundbreaking ceremony at the end of January. Mayor Langford was there and he's been a big supporter. It was just a real special moment. A lot of supporters came out. We had a big crowd. Don had to get a lot of work done before Mission Impossible got there, and he did but it wasn't quite ready. Dan Cassidy was a little frustrated because it wasn't really in a state where they could do as much as they could, but they still did a lot. It was very helpful. It was about that time that Anthony and I went to go see another donor (who desired to remain anonymous for this book). He said that he would take it under consideration. In May of '99, we were making progress but we were about out of money. We had graduation and that lady, the prophetess lady from Detroit came, and Dewayne (Coker) couldn't play that flowing music[3] (laughs). But she was prophesying all this stuff and one of the things she was prophesying was: "Anthony you need to follow what God has put on your heart…"

BOBBY: "A big decision."

BOBBY: A "big decision," and I was going, "What's that about?" Anyway, Anthony calls me after that and he wants to talk and he comes and sits in the chair over there in my office and tells me that he's going to take a position up in Franklin, Tennessee with a school. I could have fallen out of my chair. Because here I said, "We're half way into building this thing. We've got three months before a school opens. Are you sure God is telling you to do this?" He explained this to the board at the next board meeting which was Paul Pankey's first meeting. Paul likes to say (imitating Paul's shrill voice), "My first board meeting Anthony Gordon resigns. And we don't have any money and the building is half built." (Lots of laughter) We said, "Paul, we just wanted to see if you had the gumption to be a board member. This is your initiation."

BOBBY: I thought, "Boy, I know this is going to be his first and last board meeting."

BILLY: But he hung in there. It was like "Whoa!." I said, "Well, Paul, it's actually been worse than this at times."

BOBBY: Anthony said, "I'm like a quarterback that can't take another hit."

BILLY: He was telling Dee Powell, "I've been sacked too many times behind the line, and I just couldn't take another hit."

BOBBY: I think that's why we had grace for it.

BILLY: We knew what Anthony had sacrificed for eleven years.

CARL: **Jimmy Mulvaney was the first one to break the silence when Anthony said that. He said, "I've never had to face what you faced."**

BILLY: That's when Jim Pinto and I went to see (anonymous donor) a second time, and he said, "You've got yourself a bit of a situation here, don't you?" I said, "Yeah, it has been difficult." And he said, "Well, I can't really give it to you directly just for the political reasons, but I'll give $100,000 to Jim Pinto, and Jim, you know what to do with it." I said, "Thank you very much." Then we had a board meeting promoting Ron (Carter). Anthony said he'd stay until December to help the transition, and so we got that situation resolved. We got over that, but then the next issue was that we had a half-finished school, but we didn't have any money left. We had to say to Don, "Let's just take a timeout until we can figure out what we we're going to do." And we asked him how long it was going to take and Don said, "Well, if we really hump it we can probably do it in two months, at least the downstairs." Of course we didn't have the money to complete the upstairs or the downstairs at that point. I talked to Paul and Jimmy and Paul said we could talk to First Commercial Bank, and of course they weren't going to make a loan to the school. They would do it in the school's name, but they said they had to have us sign as guarantors. Paul really jumped in with both feet. He had only been a board member for about one month. He and Jimmy and I went over to First Commercial and took out a line of credit for up to $300,000, and we thought that would be enough to complete it, and we drew on that to get Don started again. We got the doors open just in time. They were working up to the last minute. We had an unbelievable commissioning ceremony for the school. Dan Cassidy came back and Mayor Langford was there and we had a big crowd. We dedicated the building and the kids were all there. We had some kids cut the ribbon. It was a wonderful day. And 164 kids piled in that downstairs.

Carl: **How have you seen Restoration Academy come to where it is now, and how has God used it in your personal walk and life?**

BOBBY: For me and Roxanne, we had a banquet that George Grant spoke at that was a fundraiser at the Café de France. The banquet at that site was sort of my brainchild and the board supported it. And I just thought that it was vision casting dinner. We weren't going to put pressure on anyone or have cards sitting on the table or anything. George toured Tuskegee the same day and he talked about that statue and it was a moving talk. There were a lot of big-wig people that came because of Reverend Barker. It was just incredible. It was going just perfect. At the end, Mr. Nasser comes up to me and says, "Who do I give this bill to?" This unbelievable and romantic vision of everything going perfect just crashed. I thought, "We don't have a penny," and I was humiliated. I looked at it and it was like for almost $4,000 and I remember pulling Roxanne over to the side and going (whispering), "How much money do we have in our checking account?" She said, "I don't know." I said, "Do we have this much?" She said, "We might have a little left over after that." I said, "Well, let me see the checkbook." I didn't even ask her because I was afraid that she was going to say no, and I wrote that check and tried to keep my composure and act like it was all supposed to be that way to Mr. Nasser. You never plan anything that way, and you never tell anybody to do it that way. It probably wasn't the right way to do it, but it was just another case of absurdity that wasn't real organized.

BILLY: Well, if you organized the event you had to figure out how to pay for it (laughs)

BOBBY: The board probably would have helped, but I was too prideful to go to them.

BILLY: I thought it was a miracle (laughing).

BOBBY: I was too prideful to tell anybody. But one thing I do remember about that is that Hank Hankerson came to that dinner, and Hank Hankerson is the one that brought Bill Lewis out to the school. So, I thought God honored that little bit I gave.

BILLY: Bill Lewis came out just in time before Anthony left and he got to meet him in December of '99. We got that first $10,000 gift because at the next board meeting everyone was going, "Who is William R. Lewis?" Nobody knew him.

BOBBY: Being on the board and being involved with Restoration Academy reminded me of my favorite quote from Chesterton. He says, "Anything worth doing is worth doing badly." Because the world I come from you're supposed to have your i's dotted and your t's crossed and everything needs to be in order. Really though, ministry is messy. And it's painful. It does take faith, I mean real faith where you are really faced with just dealing with something that on the face of it is absolutely absurd to do. And you have to discern between what's really absurd and what's faith. Because you can do things that are just reckless. I think, with all candor, probably a lot of the things we did were reckless. And I look back and I wouldn't say, "Do it this way."

BILLY: Like Ron used to say when he was the executive director, "We're trying to jack the house up to put in the foundation."

BOBBY: God uses the foolish to confound the wise, and I guess that's what I learned from it. It will always be a huge part of my life as well as the friendships I made through it all. Even though I didn't meet LaGarrius (former student) through Restoration Academy; we got him in the school and it made a big difference in his life. I could just go on and on. I think it's by far the best ministry in the city. I just think it's one of the best things of its kind in the country. Who would have ever dreamed that it is what it is today? It could wind up being a whole lot more.

BILLY: For me, if we just do our little part, God will do a giant part. That has happened over, and over, and over. I'm not a real risk taker. I like to line things up and have things organized. This has been totally the opposite from the get go. We're starting to get some order. It's night and day compared to how it used to be. The thing about this school and how it's impacted me is the realization that the best place to be is in utter dependence on God. And when you know you're doing His will and you can see Him working — like Paul Pankey says it strengthened his faith more than anything he's ever been involved in. Because you can see where we were and it was impossible. And there are verses in both the New and Old Testament that say, "With men this is not possible but with God nothing is impossible." The faith is where you can't see how it's going to happen but you know you're supposed to do it, and God says He'll bring it about. And when you get on the other side of it and you look back it kind of cements that foundation again. That's why they kept saying to the children of Israel, "You have to tell your children about what God did in the past and He'll do it again in the future." It kind of gives you a hope and a reason for your belief. When you come across a hard time in your personal life or anywhere else you know that God did what He said in this place. We were risking. Of course we weren't risking as much as all of you working there or Don Pierson building the building, but we were taking a big risk. We were crossing the Jordan.

BOBBY: I think what we really did is we embraced sharing the burden and not just the excitement of things. The burden of it, I think we embraced that. I think that's what happened at that board meeting. We said, "We're going to hug this porcupine even though we know we're going to bleed. We're going to hug it."

BILLY: Like you said, it's messy.

BOBBY: Yeah. It's messy. Hard. Painful. But unbe-
             lievably gratifying, kind of like child birth
             or something.

BILLY: It's like this beautiful child that God has
             birthed. You had a little part to do with it.
             It's a modern day miracle.

CHAPTER 5

"Coming from Nothing" with Paul Pankey

B IOGRAPHICAL SKETCH: *Paul Pankey has been on the board at Restoration Academy for almost a decade. He joined the board during one of its most chaotic and perilous years at a time when it was broke, in debt to the IRS, and without an executive director. He joined the team and never looked back. Over the years he has been a faithful giver of his time and resources. He and his wife Josephine reside in Mountain Brook.*

Carl: I've heard you share more than once how God used Restoration Academy more than anything else to grow your faith. I think a lot of people would share this sentiment. Can you explain how God has used the school in this way?

Paul: Well, I just saw the thing **come from nothing**. When I got on the board we were three hundred thousand dollars in debt and we couldn't pay the teachers. Why I stayed, I don't know. I think it was Billy's prayers. I saw the fruit of this thing grow from that dismal start to where it is today. Then the Lord sent us somebody like Bill Lewis to just really save Restoration Academy. And you can just see the Lord's hand in the whole thing. To put something like that on Bill's heart and see the fruit of those prayers come to fruition has strengthened my faith.

Carl: **What are some other ways you've seen the school come from almost nothing to something?**

Paul: Well, the thing that has really impressed me more than anything is you guys...the teachers. There were some times where we couldn't pay you. The loyalty and commitment and the mission mentality of this whole thing strengthened my faith more than anything. That and seeing the Lord just miraculously bringing forth the monetary means to support this thing.

Carl: **Over the years you've made significant contributions to the school of both your time and your treasure. You've spent a lot of time rallying other people to do the same. What is it about the school that causes you to grab someone's arm and say, "Hey, you need to come out and see what's going on at Restoration Academy?"**

Paul:

It's just to see the fruit of it. I've been on the board of probably ten Christian ministries. Some of them were fairly good, some were pretty good, but this one I'm close to rating about 95% successful. I've been on other ones that might have been 5% successful. Of all the Christian ministries that I've been involved with this is the best. It gives kids a chance at life. It's either jail or this. It's to create productive citizens out of these kids and lead them down the right path to see the Lord and everything else.

Carl:

How have you seen this ministry affect your family?

Paul:

Well, I've seen my children get involved. Tripp has given significantly to this thing. He doesn't make a whole lot of money but he gives a good bit. I think he supports one or two kids out there. I think Simmons has done that. They have a little Pankey Family LLC. They said anytime they have a closing they give approximately 10% of the proceeds to the school. We had a meeting, and I might have influenced it a bit (laughs). They all agreed that this was a good cause. They give 10% to the Lord and they choose to give most of it to Restoration Academy.

Carl:

Anything else you'd like to add here in closing?

Paul: The staff. I look at people like Connie Edwards who could make three times what she's making. You guys could make three times what you're making. The dedication of the staff has inspired me tremendously. You just can't find this anywhere else. I know other Christian schools where the teachers are just in it for the pay. The staff out there is so dedicated. I just wish that the staff at my company was as dedicated as the staff out at Restoration Academy because it's really just a privilege.

CHAPTER 6

"Walking on the Water" with Dr. Alan Carter, Sally Carter and Jimmy Mulvaney

BIOGRAPHICAL SKETCH: *Dr. Alan Carter and his wife Sally have been friends and supporters of Restoration Academy. They both served on RA's original advisory board. Dr. Carter has served at pastor of Faith Presbyterian and he and his church have been instrumental stakeholders in the life and history of the school since its inception.*

Like the Carters, Jimmy Mulvaney was a part of RA's original advisory board. He also served on RA's original working board for several years. Since that time he has faithfully given of his time and resources to help support the ministry. He is the owner of Pump and Process, and he is married with children.

Carl:	What originally drew you to Restoration Academy?
JIMMY:	I had been involved in the inner-city ministry with Young Life. I was on the

urban board of directors there. I got to spend many, many years driving around with Billy Longshore in vans.

DR. ALAN
CARTER: The infamous vans.

JIMMY: I would drive late nights down roads that I would never, never be on other than to be with these groups of kids that I was blessed to get to know. I spent a lot of time out in that area and developed a love for the community and a passion for the community. I think one of the first things that I remember thinking that the school might facilitate was really a desire I had that the kids we worked with and got to know in the community would not just want to get out and go somewhere else but stay. I saw the potential of a school being something that could really help make that happen. I had a respect for African-Americans who had come up in tough areas like that and who had an opportunity to go somewhere else and then came back or stayed and had a passion for their community. I remember thinking that a school may help facilitate that. As far as the draw, the biggest draw was Billy Longshore and seeing Billy's passion for that place. It was just contagious for me and I think for a lot of people.

DR. CARTER: Mine was a little different. I was raised a racist in Mississippi in the 1960s. I

became a Christian in 1970 and when I
began to understand that the ground at the
foot of the Cross was level that began to
change my attitudes about a lot of things.
All varieties of Pharisaism you might
say. I began to wonder why conservative
Presbyterian churches in the South would
spend thousands and thousands of dollars
sending missionaries to Africa but weren't
doing anything among black people in the
United States in the cities they were in. It
seemed like an enormous disjunction. I
moved here in 1986 after a graduate school
experience. It took me a few years to get
my pastoral head screwed on. I thought
God had been guiding me into teaching.
My avenue into the school actually came
through Anthony Gordon. I don't know
when in the timeline of Restoration
Academy, Anthony came into the PCA
(Presbyterian Church of America). But
when he came into the PCA, I remember
that day in the presbytery thinking, "Hey,
a black man. This is good. We need this
badly." So I sought Anthony out after that
and just said basically, "Let's have lunch.
I want to get to know you." I followed
that up with another lunch between him,
me and at least one other elder from
this church. I think Johnny Johnson was
the man. And we, I guess by the grace
of God, we didn't show up saying to
Anthony: "We know how to fix your
ministry." But we basically said, "We
feel like God... like there's an obligation

on us to do something in the city and we would like to explore opportunities of ways we might be able to do that." And you know, he could have said "Yeah, we need money, money, money" or whatever and I probably would have gone and tried to get it. But he began by saying, "Well you know if we can develop a sense of brotherhood first..." These are maybe not his exact words but something like this, "Then maybe we could explore opportunities and ways that your church could be involved." I was pretty impressed by that answer. This white Over-the-Mountain guy sitting here basically saying I could help him, and he didn't immediately go to my pocketbook, but went to my heart. I can't give you a lot of steps after that. I was convinced then, and I'm convinced now, that there are lots and lots and lots of resources, people resources, all kinds of resources over the mountain that want to get involved with helping in the city but don't know how. Don't know where to grab a hold of this thing that looks so big. They're looking for a ministry, a person, a group that they can trust and partner with. Our vision as a church is to help people in Birmingham and throughout the world find their joy in Jesus rather than their joy in stuff, and power, and possessions, and prestige and all that kind of stuff. If we are going to be faithful in seeking to accomplish that vision, we've got to have partners - because there's only a few hundred of us and we can't do the whole job. And so over time we did develop a sense of brotherhood I think with Anthony and I think there was a gap actually between my initial seeking of Anthony out and getting involved with the board. I remember we had him speak in the church a couple of times... I tell people I'm past 50, I can't sequence anymore...

SALLY
CARTER: He was preaching!

DR. CARTER: Yeah, he was preaching. He came one Sunday night and I said, "Look, why don't you preach about 15 minutes and take questions for about 15 minutes - because, while I'm interested in the word being taught, I want people to find out about the ministry." So he preached for 15 minutes and was just getting going and he said, "Well, Dr. Carter says I have to stop now and so I'm going to take your questions." Boy, I still hear about that. But actually I do think there was some kind of a gap there and all of a sudden I got this call that there was a board being formed. I don't know where that happened on the timeline. But anyway, I got this call to come be on this board, this initial board. And we met. This was when Billy's office was down at Park Place Tower, I think. We went down there and man, those were different days. Those were different days.

Sally and I were talking; I never visited the school when it was on Division Street.

SALLY: Because he had gotten interested in this, then that's how I got interested. At the time, I was working at Briarwood in their elementary library - and had been there for five years maybe. I had been kind of tapering off on that. It was just 20 hours a week and I got down to 10 hours a week. I can't exactly remember how it happened but when they moved to a new building, I know I went over there with my son Tim and we painted the ceiling in the room that Carl used to teach in.

CARL: **There was a lot of scraping and painting in that building.**

SALLY: There was, but it needed it. I remember one room was purple. DARK purple... but they got it up and going.

CARL: **The library you started was maybe the size of a closet. It was half the size of this room.**

SALLY: But, I started thinking: When I first started working at Briarwood, there was not much money being put into it but as the years went by, they started getting that library in better shape. They were pouring money into it. And I thought...

CARL: **You're talking about the Briarwood library?**

SALLY: Yes, Briarwood... and I thought: "They've got what they need, but these poor kids over here, they haven't got anything." So I said something to Anthony about starting a library and he found me this little closet room, and Caroline Poythress and Ruth Radbill both volunteered to help me. We got books donated and we got people to donate money and we bought books and we scrounged together some shelves. We had our little library and the kids would come by. One day a week each class would come by and we would read to them and give the teachers a break.

CARL: **What are some key moments that solidified your belief in the significance of the ministry, your commitment to it, and that God was in it.**

JIMMY: My, I'm over 50 now ... so my memory gets hazy. I'll try to throw out a few bullet points, that'll probably be the best I can do. I remember there being an older lady, a grandmother, whose son had seen a friend of his killed. He had seen it happen on the street and this lady came and was basically in the process of begging Anthony to take her grandson into the school.

DR. CARTER: And you were there?

JIMMY: Yes. I think it was in Anthony's office
                  back at the church campus.

JIMMY: It shook me to the core because I remember
                  thinking: "I have never, and probably
                  will never know the emotions that this
                  lady had." Growing up and living, as you
                  said, Over the Mountain. That just etched
                  ... that was like a brand on me that never
                  went away - just seeing that and being a
                  part of that. Because I had heard Anthony
                  talk about the stories of the kids who'd
                  seen their friends killed. I think that was
                  almost commonplace for Anthony, that
                  type of tragedy ... just being there for that
                  and seeing that, and sensing the fear and
                  the desperation that this grandma had for
                  her grandson ... just realizing how other-
                  worldly this was for me. That's surreal,
                  I mean, I see stuff like that on TV some-
                  times but this really, you know, this really
                  does happen, doesn't it? Of course I'd
                  seen it being involved with the commu-
                  nity, working with gangs and having to
                  take knives out of gang members' hands
                  and guns out of dads' hands getting ready
                  to kill their son or threatening to do it.
                  That's the moment that stands out the
                  most.

DR. CARTER: That right there reminds me of a word
                  that Anthony used to use all the time and
                  what that grandmother lacked was advo-
                  cacy. She didn't have an advocate and you
                  see that desperation. We know advocacy,

we know people with power and we have
money and you can avoid certain problems with those things. Anthony used to
talk about how we need people to be an
advocate.

Wow, key things that drew me in. I
was really impressed. It's related to the
kind of thing that Jimmy's talking about.
I was really impressed with Anthony's
story. I mean everybody's heard it, about
why he originally started the school.
Those funerals he did within - I don't
know - three funerals within six weeks or
something like that. That was impressive,
but I don't have a lot of magic moments.
I'm not sure I have any. Frankly I'm not
the kind of guy that's motivated that way.
Anthony made the statement, "I get them
an hour or two a week, the school's got
them thirty or so hours a week. Where
am I going to come out in this deal?" I
mean, that's just right. That's not a magic
moment really, but that's just right. You
just need more contact in everything. I
guess it also drew me in just to think I
could help make a difference. Not in a
major league way. I'm the kind of person
that's attracted to the underdogs and boy
Restoration sure was, you may say still
is, some people say still is. I don't know,
if Restoration is an underdog now, it was
an underdog to the tenth power back in
those days. And that may say something
weird about me, but I'm attracted to that.
There's another large Christian urban

school that got started somewhere a long the way after Restoration got started and they were well-heeled, at least from my perspective they were, and a deal like that, they didn't need me. But I really think Anthony's heart for the whole thing was the main attractive thing for me. Sally got to know a lot of the kids individually and personally by being in the library. I would have loved to have heard the kind of thing you were just talking about, Jimmy. But I didn't ever witness anything like that. I don't have a lot of magic moments.

CARL: **That's sounds pretty magic to me, the relationships, that's good. I think that's part of the deal.**

SALLY: I remember when I was over painting. My son Tim and I were out washing our brushes. It might have been one of Anthony's kids, maybe his younger one, and some other kids; they were out playing around the school building. They were playing that they were involved in a drive-by shooting. (Pause) And they were making loud popping sounds using balloons or something. That was a magic moment. It sure helped me to see the need - that this is where these kids are living. This is every day for them. The other thing that drew me in was getting to be with them, with the kids, and read with them and see their little faces sparkle and the lights come on and see them want to come back and check out a book. That was one of my goals; to get them fired up about reading. Anytime you can see a child get excited about checking out a book, that's exciting. (Pause) They can't read the Bible if they can't read.

CARL: **How have you seen the school grow and develop from the time you got involved until today?**

JIMMY: My heart was there. I got involved with the board. One of the things that I kind of fell into was somewhat of a faculty advocate, if you will. God just gives us all different gifts and abilities. My focus was obviously on kids ultimately, but I just felt called to get some things done pretty quickly as far as the staff goes. I remember going to board meetings and having certain objectives to bring up and most of them were related to the faculty. I heard at the second board meeting that the faculty had no health insurance. I really… I remember… anger is not the word, just disgust, is what it was. I just thought how in the world can we use the word holistic … how in the world can we have a ministry here … how in the world can we want to minister to these kids and teach these kids and not take care of the people that are doing it? I remember thinking: "What's going to happen… what are we as a board going to do if, God forbid, one of the children of one of the teachers gets some kind of bad disease? How are they going to be taken care of?" I just thought "This is ridiculous." So I said first things first. I remember, I said to the board if it means us having twenty or thirty less students next year, I think we need to have health insurance. I said, as a matter of fact, I'm just going to pay for it. I'm going to pay for it, and if I can get paid back, great, and if not... but I don't want to be on a board and be over these teachers in any way if we can't take care of them. I can't in good conscience expect them to not be able to take care of their families. Anyway it was just something that I guess the Lord used me to bring it to the board's attention because there wasn't anybody that argued against it certainly. In some ways it was: "Hey, you know, (scratching heads) yeah, we do need to do that."

DR. CARTER: I think most of us didn't know...

JIMMY: Yeah, maybe we didn't, maybe we didn't.

SALLY: We were struggling to even pay them a monthly salary.

CARL: **Who would argue with "They need it, I'll pay for it?" (laughs)**

JIMMY: I wasn't Mr. Moneybags by any stretch of the imagination and I'll go into what

I'll speak about next, but I just thought that's just something we've got to do. Those were some fun days, but one day Billy called and said, "We've just been told that we've got to be out of our church building." And I said "What do you mean by that, Billy?" He said "Well, we've got to leave. The school has to leave. We can't have the school there." What did he say? "Eighteen months, or seventeen months... and we're gone?" We didn't have, as you mentioned earlier, we didn't have a deep pocketed board and we didn't have a lot of fundraisers that were well underway. We didn't have an income. As you said, we struggled to pay teachers. Month to month it was a struggle every month. Billy and I were faced with the reality that somebody needed to... we needed to build a new school. We needed to have a place to go. The only thing we could do really was build our own place. Billy and I were faced with the fact that we needed to put our names on a $300,000 dollar loan. At the time, I had only just recently started my business (laughter) and I was actually not ... I had let everybody on the board know I had my own struggles. I wasn't poor and I was eating, but month to month was tough for me in a way. But I had a little bit of equity in a couple things, not a whole lot. I'm a worse-case thinker, as an engineer, I remember thinking, what if Anthony... you hear wild stories; there are Ted Haggard stories everywhere unfortunately... "What if Anthony you know, runs off and just disappears and the school's no more?" We build the school and something happens. Because being liable, I wasn't liable for half, I was liable for the whole thing. That's the way that works. And God just took that away from me. It was an incredible opportunity for me to make a step of faith unlike any I ever had because literally I would have been ruined. I mean, there's no way I could have come up with that if something happened and I needed to pay it.

DR. CARTER: Good economic times. (Laughs)

JIMMY: Oh yeah, great economic times. But you talk about a test of faith for me and I called several people, godly men and women and asked them. I sought counsel; I didn't just do it flippantly. I really sought counsel and I wanted to be a good steward of what God had given me and I knew what the answer was going to be. But I did want to go through those and make sure I was being led by God and not being pushed by emotion or anything else, but completely led by God to do this. And I was. And now I want to say that my second biggest sin in my life is pride. As a man, I think everybody can assume what my first biggest sin is. Another thing I want to make sure now is that I want to take no glory. God did this completely. I was a scared weenie. I did this... I was trembling the whole time I did it. I'd love to say, "Yeah, I do this and I'm going to trust God for it." Like I said, I wanted to be led by God but I sought counsel and maybe I subconsciously was hoping somebody would say. "Jimmy, don't do it. You're crazy if you do it. Tell them to find another way." But God didn't give me an out.

SALLY: Nobody said that.

JIMMY: Nobody.

DR. CARTER: How many names were on that note? Just you and Billy?

JIMMY: Yeah, Billy and I. And I remember, I'm not a finance guy. I have technical background and that's the first time I heard if you put your name on a note like that, you're not just liable for half, you're liable for the whole thing.

CARL: Let's talk about that, and don't feel like you have to give a chronology on this, but something that sticks out in terms of the way you've seen the school develop over the years. In terms of its ability to accomplish its mission, how it's matured.

DR. CARTER: Wow, it's matured and developed fiscally, financially. I remember going to the board meetings at Billy's and I remember going to the board meetings in Fairfield. It just seemed like every board meeting was a financial crisis. Literally, every board meeting. We were meeting every two weeks, sometimes every week. But they were not monthly meetings, it was just always financial crisis which just rattled my cage.

JIMMY: I think we all took it personally. We didn't just get up there and go: "That's the school and the school's problems." Those were our problems.

DR. CARTER: I will be completely candid about all this. I do think with all that Anthony brought to the table, Anthony at least in the early days, did not work well with the board. There were a lot of things we didn't know that I thought we should have known. Like the health thing. Like some debt that we found out about all of the sudden one time.

Carl: **Yeah, when I started. And let me interject, this may help. When the board started, it was "an advisory board" and it kind of developed into a working board.**

DR. CARTER: Right, I was going to mention that because I remember asking Billy one time, I said, "Billy, what is our legal liability here? Do we have officers and directors and such?" I mean, seriously. I just didn't know where we were. I thought they might be coming back to me or coming back to my church because I kind of represent the church. It was an advisory board and I remember going to Billy one time and he said, "Well, I don't really know. That's so funny, it's kind of undefined." And I thought, "Well, OK," Frank Barker has this saying "If you're walking on the water, taking another step ain't so bad. It's getting out of the boat the first time." And so we were kind of **walking on the water**. I tell you another way I think the school has really changed: If you had asked Anthony at one juncture is the school a ministry or an educational institution, he would have said it's a ministry. Not in any kind of big way and I certainly hope not in any kind of an obnoxious way, I had the opinion that if we were not successful as a school, we could not be successful as a ministry. I remember that coming sort of to a head at a planning retreat that was held at Briarwood. I beat the drums I had chosen to beat.

CARL: **I was there.**

DR. CARTER: Part of the growth and development of the school is the growth and development of Carl Lynn. That's another subject I guess. But I remember meeting you and who you were then as a young Birmingham-Southern graduate and who you are now. That's a big part of what's happened. I get thrilled when I hear the presentations you make. In my opinion, you do a really excellent job.

Anyway, there was a meeting... there were a couple of them. I remember a meeting or two that I attended at the Civil Rights Institute. (Carl) or somebody made a comment and I could tell, "Hey, they're really seeking to be a school." And that's been a change. That's been, in my view, a maturation, growth and development kind of a thing. That from my perspective is good. I won't downplay any of the ministry aspect. A man that taught me Christian education at a reformed seminary in the early, mid 1970s used to say, "If you're not seeking to be an excellent school, you're defaming the name of Christ." And I thought, "Hey that's right." The school has grown in that way, markedly, definably. I've just been thrilled at some of the things I've heard and seen lately.

There were all kinds of other things happening along the way. Like when Ben Sciacca got involved, when Joey Braddock got involved and moved out there. And others like that. I've seen the faculty grow and develop.

I'll tell you one little story that probably helped a lot, more than I realize. It was probably the second building program out there. Somebody asked me to lead something - some kind of prayer effort - and I think I had the wisdom to say Barbara Barker needs to do that, not me. They asked Barbara and she did it. I think, again, you can answer this better than me, but I think it made a lot of difference. Getting her involved and some other people...

CARL: **She's never left.**

DR. CARTER: That's not exactly growth and development but it is in the sense of how many people are now involved. Man those other days, Jimmy, it was scary. I mean, no offense on you and Billy and me and anybody else, but man... I mean, Paul Pankey wasn't involved in those days. I look at the masthead today and honestly I don't know most of those guys. In the early days it was kind of like: "What are we doing?" (Laughs)

JIMMY: You had mentioned Doc, that Anthony didn't work well with the board... well he didn't know *how* to work with the board. We didn't know how to work with Anthony...

DR. CARTER: I agree, I'm not hurling big stones along the way...

JIMMY: I know you weren't...

DR. CARTER: I just kind of wanted to put that out there that none of us knew what we were doing. There was no map, was there?

JIMMY:

None at all. I think that in response to your question ... Restoration Academy stands out to me unlike any ministry I've been involved with or heard about, read about, observed. A lot of places say, "Come out and see who we are and give us your money." Restoration Academy says "Come out, see who we are... love to have your money... but we want you. We want you to stay here. We want you to come teach the kids if you can. We want you to get involved in this place." That's why my brother Michael now is feeling compelled to get involved. He feels like you guys don't want his money, you want him. You guys have done a fabulous job, a fabulous job of doing that. To me that's one of the ways that it's grown, it's changed, it's developed... just the method by which we support, by which the school is supported. Unlike us sitting around ... "Where is this going to come from, how are we going to pay?" These guys have metamorphosed into ... it's a fabulous ministry not just to these kids but to everybody that comes out. To me, I tell people all the time. "Look, it's easy to give this place money." I see these teachers, especially in the early days and I know now, too, making next to nothing, sacrificing their lives. These guys (Ben and Carl), both of which could have a job making over a hundred thousand dollars a year working for Bellsouth, have committed their lives and their families to this place. Just the tools that God's given them and everybody out there, I mean Ty, and everybody... it's so corny and cliché to say it but "a family." Come out and be a part of this place. Don't just come and see, come and be a part, and stay, meta-phorically, in many ways. I know another big Christian school here in town, and I'll mention this here, they are a money machine. But I don't sense the emotion; I don't sense the ownership that a lot of different people feel in that place that they do here.

DR. CARTER: I actually think that goes back, there's a marked difference between that and some other different ministries but your comment reminded me of Anthony's heart in my first meeting with him - when he said "Let's develop a brotherhood and then we'll see if we can work together." I do think the seeds of that were there early on.

JIMMY: That's just trickled down and continues today.

DR. CARTER: That's really the way ministry is supposed to be.

JIMMY: That's right. It's almost like the Spirit of God is there with that, it's still there within these guys.

DR. CARTER: Without Restoration Academy I wouldn't know Jimmy, I wouldn't have known Paul Pankey, and a whole host of other people. That's part of the blessing, isn't it? I just think it's thrilling to be around people that God is moving in the way he's moving in. That's a big blessing in the whole thing. I guess it's a semi-selfish kind of thing.

SALLY: Well, the same thing. I don't think it's anything new. Just the teachers and the staff that God has brought together, just dedicated people that have changed the whole atmosphere and you can see the kids change in it as a result. I've watched ya'll deal with people that are not easy to deal with. Be firm with them until they finally get where they start to catch on, start to figure out.

CARL: You walked the halls for years. In terms of the atmosphere, how have you seen it hopefully grow and mature or change in any way?

SALLY: From the early days, I remember a lot of spankings... spankings, spankings, spankings. But they weren't very hard, they were very light. I mean some days it was just nonstop. I don't think it was really helping a whole lot. I've seen that evolve to where the discipline situation has turned around somewhat. And I would say that it's more in a positive way. That's one example.

CARL: I want you to kind of speak on a macro level a little bit, but how it's blessed your church. You've talked to me a lot about the benefit of Restoration Academy and how it's blessed your people. And then Jimmy, if you want to talk about your family, your extended family, how you've seen it impact them.

DR. CARTER: We need you guys at least as much as you need us. There is no doubt about that. We're about to have an outreach conference. Missionaries and the ministries ... they are the have-nots and we are the haves. They're coming and bringing their dog and pony show and if we like their dog and pony show, we'll give them some money and we'll bless them. God will use us to bless them. I just think that that's an incredibly mad way to look at the whole process. One of the things I'm constantly telling our whole church is what we are about. We're about the glory of God. There's just no doubt about it. How is God going to be glorified? God's going to be glorified as I said earlier, when we find our joy in Jesus rather than other things and we're trying to export that. We're trying to influence people with that locally and globally and everywhere in between and we can't do it all. And I would just say that if God is calling us to be faithful in word-based and deed-based ministries, then we've got to have partners.

Another thing I'm constantly telling people is the world tells you the way to have a blessed life is to be served, to consume goods and services, to go for all the gusto you can, to serve yourself. The Bible says, "No! The way to have a happy and blessed and joyful life is to die to self and serve other people." Those two are polar opposites. Jesus takes the world's wisdom and He just turns it upside down. Of course it takes faith to do that. Who are the most blessed people at Faith Presbyterian church? They are the people that serve the most, the people that die to self the most, the people that get involved the most. Going back to something Jimmy said, "Yeah, these guys could be earning over $100,000 at Bellsouth or some other places," and their response might be: "I want more joy than that. I want more out of life than that."

So we need you guys. We've got an obligation to this city how are we going to do that? We've got to have partners. We've got to have partners. We really need to, in the next year or two, we need to think very seriously about planting a church somewhere in the city, where the word is not like it ought to be. Because that is God's calling on our life. We will be blessed. That's the way it works. I mean, you don't do it for yourself, you just find out: "He who seeks to save his life will lose it, he who loses his life for my sake and the gospel's will find it." So if we want life, we've got to give ourselves away. The media is constantly saying, "Don't give yourself away." The media is saying, "Hold onto yourself, pamper yourself, live for yourself. And everything that comes to you, you deserve it, consume it, buy it. You'll be happy if you buy our product, if you use this, if you eat that, if you go here." Jesus just cuts through all that. I'm not saying there's anything bad about going on vacation, you know, I enjoy that. But fulfillment in your soul comes from dying to self and serving other people.

JIMMY: I think as far as how it's impacted me and my family, the thing that comes to mind first and foremost is that we have an enemy and the enemy wants us to be sedentary and comfortable and apathetic and addicted to mediocrity. I'm guilty in so many ways of all of that. What Restoration Academy does for my family is it's given us an opportunity from the talks that we have with my children, and from them hearing me pray for you guys, and for the students and for the teachers ... and hearing other people talk about my involvement over the years and also my objectives for them over the next few years, to get them involved and take them out there because they are the age now where it's perfect for them. It's a vehicle through which I can show my family we need to leave, just like Jesus did, just like Paul did, just like the disciples did ... nothing ever happened in Christ's ministry, or the ministry of His disciples by them sitting – nobody came to them. They went. Restoration Academy is a place for my family to go – we don't *have* to go to Africa, we don't have to go to anywhere else. We can go 10 miles down the road into another world and get out of our comfort zone and experience cultural shock in some ways, but also just see the ways much of the rest of the other world lives. What I can do as father of my children is pray that God uses Restoration Academy as just one start, plain and simple, in developing a worldview, not just Birmingham, not just their little school, their private school that they're in, the holy huddle that we stay in – life under a basket. There are so many ways that Restoration Academy has and can continue to facilitate this reality to my family.

DR. CARTER: That ties into what I said, you're saying you need them.

JIMMY: Oh, absolutely, absolutely. Hey listen, I tell people all the time that come to me, people going to the mission field: "Would you consider investing in my ministry?" I say, "Listen, first I want to be clear about this, I'd hate to do what you do. I'd hate to have to go to people and ask ... but I want to tell you from my perspective, it is a blessing to me for you to ask me that. It keeps me off my butt. Thank you for the opportunity you are giving me to see my family blessed by me giving to you. To be blessed by the Holy Spirit. To give to you, you're creating opportunities." Sometimes people get a little bit of spark in their eyes like they'd never thought of that before. And you guys need to remember that. It's about the kids first but it's also about the families and the people that ya'll draw in - the opportunity that they have to be blessed by God by giving of themselves and their resources and everything else. It's just the way it's supposed to work.

CHAPTER 7

"Jacking Up the House" with Ron Carter

BIOGRAPHICAL SKETCH: *Ron Carter came to Restoration Academy in 1998 and served as principal under Dr. Anthony Gordon, the founder. He came on the staff as a "principal in training" and devoted his early time to teaching high school Bible and humanities courses. After Dr. Gordon stepped down as Executive Director in 1999, Ron Carter assumed the reins. He served as director when the school transitioned from Eastlake to Fairfield. He served as Executive Director until 2003. At that point he took a position with DeVos Ministries working as part of their Urban Initiative. He is still with DeVos today. He and his wife and his two children reside in Helena.*

BEN:	Talk to me about your introduction to Restoration Academy and how you got involved.
RON:	Prior to coming to Restoration, I was at Children's Aid Society and I was running this program called Project Dads. I was

also in seminary out at Briarwood taking some classes. I remember one day at class that Bobby Nix caught me right before class started and asked me to come out into the hallway. I did and he just kind of real quickly asked me "Have you ever thought about being a principal?" I said, "A principal of what?" He said, "I really can't go into much detail but we may have a need for a principal at the Academy and your name came up." I responded by saying "Well, you realize I don't really have a degree in education." He said, "Well, we know. That's really not a big issue for us. We're basically looking for someone who's going to be loyal to Anthony and to the board so we'll talk about it later." I had no idea exactly what was going down. I found out later what was going on with the existing principal at the time. And one thing kind of led to another. I met with Anthony and he kind of told me what his vision was and again we re-engaged the whole idea about the fact that I didn't have a degree. He said, "Well that's OK, don't worry about it." What he laid out in the proposal was that if everything worked out he would bring me on as a, for lack of a better word, as a principal-in-training where I would sit under his tutelage for three years, and I would have a teaching role as well. Of course we didn't define what that would mean at the time, but I would be in the classroom and also handle the day-to-day administration of the school. This would go on for three years, but after three years was over; he would give me the full authority to run the day-to-day operations of the school. I was kind of at a place in my life where I sensed that it was time to make a switch. I had been at the other position for close to three years and I had a real keen interest in Christian education. I thought that the idea was kind of crazy enough that it might be God and so I met with Billy and with Anthony and we had lunch somewhere on the Southside. That's when they fully explained the idea. I think the biggest challenge for me was with the whole thing about the insurance and how that would work. I had a real peace about it though and God had really prepared me for making the transition. When I finally started working, I had the principal duties and I also taught English, Bible, and history to 11th and 12th graders.

BEN: **What were your emotions or what are some of the things that get conjured up in your mind when you think about the first couple of times at the school, walking around and seeing how it operated?**

RON: It was like the old adage: *It was the best of times, it was the worst of times* in a lot of ways. Because of my background, and because of how I'm wired, I like things that exist in order and I think one of the first things that I looked for when I got to the school was policy manuals and things like that. I searched and searched, and I asked Ms. Dozier and she just kind of shrugged her shoulders and said, "Well, you need to talk to Dr. Gordon about that." I remember right around the time I started there was an ACSI convention here in town, and I went. I think Carl went too, and Anthony and I were in a class. We had a seminar together and when it was over we were walking around and I said, "Hey, Doc (Gordon), where's the policy manual?" He said, "Well you know we just have never gotten around to doing that." I said, "Well don't you think we need some policies in place? We need a policy manual. What about contracts for the teachers." Of course his response was that he held off on being so rigid, so to speak, and not having the policy manuals and the contracts was because sometimes he couldn't fulfill his obligations to the teachers as far as being able to make payment in a timely manner. While I understood that, I never let it go. I still pressed for the policies and things like that, but then he told me, "Now you can go ahead and get it in order, but at the same time I want you to understand my rational." I said, "Yeah, that's cool, that's fine." Around that same time I had befriended Vernard (Gant) and he had left Cornerstone by that time and I would periodically meet with him and talk shop. I mentioned the policies and stuff and he said, "You know, I got it all right here." Because when the school first started, Vernard and his wife, Cynthia, had both worked at the school. She was over the data. She was the principal and she put together a whole manual and student handbook, faculty manual, all that stuff. He had it all in binders and on the shelf right above his office at home, and he also made copies of the entire manuals and had it on floppy disk for me at that time. So I just went about redoing all those things and reformatting them for Restoration Academy, and I think it was a significant point for the school in making a transition to where it is today and laying a foundation for it.

We also had to battle philosophically about what the school was because I remember one of the first things that we did when I went on staff is that me and Carl and Doc went through a strategic planning workshop with this thing called the Arrow. I remember one of the distinct battles we had and it was heated. It was primarily between Anthony and Alan Carter, and it was about whether or not Restoration was a school or was it a ministry. Doc was really, really sticking to the point that it was a ministry and Alan was like: "No, you're a school." I really didn't know, and so I joined with Doc. They went back and forth. I think

Alan's point was until you reconcile what this is, then it's not going to be able to move forward because it's a school and you've got to start acting and functioning like a school. At the time, of course, I sided with Anthony. I finally went to Covenant College, and the three years at Covenant really changed my philosophy and my whole outlook on what the school was, and what I settled on philosophically was that Restoration was a school that had a ministry emphasis to it. That really kind of set the tone for us with things like pursuing accreditation and putting things in place structurally. Often times I would illustrate it that when we first got there, Restoration was a free-standing building so to speak, but you had to **jack the building up and lay the foundation** because the way it was built, the foundation really didn't get laid like it really needed to be done. We had to go back and do the really arduous work of laying the foundation when the building was already standing and kind of my primary role was to help put that stuff in place. As I look back over my life, that's kind of what I've done. I've never been the visionary. I come along and put stuff in place. I remember when I first got there the verse God gave to me (to make) some sense of why I was there was the passage where Paul told Titus "that the reason I left you in Crete was for you to set in order things that were lacking." That's what God spoke to me and said, "That's your purpose here ... to set in order things that are lacking and once that happens, you're out." That's also when I felt like it was time for me to leave when I felt like I had done what I needed to do, and it was time to release it and let somebody else take it to the next level. So I had no hang ups about turning it loose.

BEN: **What are some stories... as far as highlights, low points, things you look back on?**

RON: There were many of those. I remember Restoration was a roller-coaster for me. I had these immense highs, but then I would have these immense lows and the lows would come from when we had to dismiss a student from the school. It didn't matter to me what the circumstances were. I remember in one case, one young man in Mr. Shep's class in the 4th grade, made an error in judgment. He brought - I'm not sure if it was a pellet pistol or something along those lines - but it was some type of weapon that he had brought to school, and it went off in his bag. By that time things were changing in the public school spectrum, especially about stuff around making threats, weapons, and stuff like that. If you brought a knife, if you brought a gun, anything that could do bodily harm or injury, there were no questions, it was just automatic out. We just couldn't run

the risk and I remember this young man
- we all liked him. When Shep came and
got me, I remember going back to the
office because I knew what was going to
have to happen. I put my face on the desk
and I wept like a baby. He just brought
me a tissue. That happened a number of
times. It happened so many times that
they started calling me Jeremiah. They
were calling me the weeping prophet. I
was just so connected to these kids, especially the guys, and wanted them to make
it so bad and knowing for a lot of them,
that was the end of the road as far as
schooling was concerned. They had come
to the school because they got kicked out
of public school, because they'd gotten in
trouble or got in gangs and their parents
were doing the best that they could.

There were also just those moments
in the classroom where you'd see a light
bulb will go on and some kid getting it
... and just some of the strange looks. I
would go into class doing some whacked
out stuff. I remember at the time I was
reading some stuff by Howard Hendricks
- *The Law of the Learner, The Law of
the Teacher* - and stuff like that. One of
the things that he talked about is going
into the classroom and just going off the
docks in your approach. I took a cue from
him and I went into the class one day and
after I called roll, I went: "Hey guys! Hey
guys! Guess what? Guess what?" They
were looking around like: *What is going*

on with him? I leaned forward and I said, "I'm glad you're here." They looked like: *"What?"* I would do stuff like that and it started catching on with the kids.

One day, this student named Nick - he wasn't a constant problem but every now and then I had to take him out in the hall - I was about to paddle him and we got to talking. I just listened to him and he just stopped in midstream and looked at me and said, "Where'd you come from?" I said, "What do you mean?" He said, "Where'd you come from? I been at this school three or four years and not one teacher has ever told me that they were glad I was here. Where you come from?" It was those kind of moments that really made it easier for me at the end of the day to have a sense of fulfillment. Of course there were some challenging moments. When students just no matter what you do (are) always trying to cut class, and smoke behind the bus, and kids thinking they can outsmart parents.

I remember one case, a guy named Connie was always kind of my antagonist in the classroom. We liked each other, but we always butted heads with each other. We were always getting into it about something. The kids knew I was kind of like Perry Mason; I could figure stuff out, and I could press them. One student, named Erin, wasn't at school and I knew something was not right. Erin's grandmother called and she didn't know where she was, and to make a long story short, I kept pressing the kids. I called them in one by one and I would interrogate them and they would try to pretend like they didn't know. One of them broke and told me that she was at Connie's house. I called Connie's mother and his mother worked at the Social Security building and she said, "No, she's not there, I'm sure." And I said, "I'm heading to your house; meet me over there." Sure enough when we got over there, she went downstairs and they were down there because Connie lived downstairs, and I had those kinds of adventures.

It was wild, but I think probably one of the most memorable experiences I had in the classroom was when we did a segment on church history. We did a lot of talking about architectural designs and worldview and things like that. You would think these kids wouldn't be interested in things like that, but it absolutely blew me away. I did this segment on architectural and medieval churches and having the floor plan of a medieval cathedral and how it was laid out in the sign of a cross. We talked about the stained glass windows, and then I did a field trip with the kids and we went and visited the historic Presbyterian church over on the Southside. We went and visited St. Mary's Episcopal church on the Southside, that United Methodist church that's in part of 5 Points South. The whole time, they went and took us around. The kids had already been taught by me about what to look for and then when the rector's came in and gave insight on the church, they were able to ask all these poignant questions and stuff. They were really engaged in it and that was a real important learning point for me as a highlight.

Lastly, the trips. When I did the black college tours, they were significant trips. They turned a lot of kids around. I remember the last one I did. I took them up to Tennessee, to Fisk, and Tennessee State. A lot of the boys they were whining and complaining: "I don't want to go. I don't know why you're making us go." But then when they got up there, their tunes totally changed and they all wanted to go to college at that point. Most of them at least attempted it for a little while.

The end of the month was always a challenging part for me as it was for Anthony because you didn't realize how much money you were going to have to pay the staff. I would have my triage sessions. I would call them in one by one and find out who was most critical and whoever was most critical was who got paid first. Now when Anthony left, one of the things he told the board and told me and Carl was to "make sure they get paid first" But I couldn't do it. I just couldn't do it. I always put myself at the back. Most of them don't know this. Even Carl doesn't know for the most (part), but I never would get paid first. I would pay him and I would pay the staff and I would get paid last because I just couldn't ... the teachers were, you know ... and it didn't hurt that I was out of debt at the time (laughing), but I just couldn't do it. Probably the low part for me every month was really struggling through: "How you gonna make payroll. Are we going to have enough?" - And looking at the faces of the teachers after they poured out themselves for a whole month of teaching and making sacrifices. And all of them could have been making money elsewhere and they were sacrificing to work at the school. That was a hard part for me-not being able to pay them on time every single month.

TY WILLIAMS: **I think this is a good segue to talk a little bit if you can about what I think was a pivotal point in the school's history and that is the Bill Lewis experience.**

RON: That was a very interesting situation. We were about to get out for Christmas break that year. I think it was around 2000. It was right at the end of the day and it was chaos. Kids were running all over the place and we were just trying to get them out and get them gone for the day, and lo and behold I look up and here comes Hank Hankerson with this guy and his wife and he said, "I wanted to bring this guy over to take a look at the school." And I really

wasn't that focused. I said, "OK, alright."
We did a tour of the school. I took them
upstairs first just to let them look for the
most part. It wasn't completed at that
time. It was aesthetic; but that was it. He
walked through and then we came back
down to my office. His wife never said a
word during the entire thing. We sat and I
told him a little bit about the background
of the school and he asked a couple of
questions and they were out. Well, during
the holidays I was periodically going
over to the school to check mail and just
make sure things were OK. This particular day, I had gone off to the school and
checked the mail, gone into the building
and was just going to put the mail on Mrs.
Dozier's desk and the phone rang while I
was there. I picked it up and it was Hank
and we chit-chatted for a few minutes
and he asked me: "Ron, are you sitting
down?" I said, "Why, do I need to be?"
He said, "Yeah, I think you do." He said,
"Do you remember that guy that I brought
out about a week ago?" I said, "Yes." He
said, "Well, he wants to make a donation to the school." ... and you'll have
to forgive me but I can't even remember
exactly how much money it was. I think
the first time it was like $300,000, which
was like a million to me at that time. I
was like: "You have got to be kidding
me." The first person I called was Billy
and we both were singing the praises of
the Lord. With that money we were able

to finish the top floor; which I think at that time cost between $150,000 and $200,000, and then we had the $100,000 in reserve which went a very, very long way (laughs). So that was significant and from that, I would periodically call him. I didn't really know who this man was and I would periodically call him and go out to lunch and just listen to him talk. Found him out to be a fascinating guy to listen to and found out what his background was. I was pretty shocked to find out he had grown up in poverty himself down in Mobile. He grew up in the projects. That kind of broke the ice a whole, whole lot.

We just had this relationship where I'd go pick him up and we'd go eat and he'd vent. He'd berate the government and George Bush and everyone else you know. But he had a genuine heart for helping what he would call "the least of these" and the downtrodden, and he made his money advocating on behalf of individuals who were oppressed, especially with the black lung stuff. And the Lord rewarded him for it. He's a very generous man. That's kind of how the relationship started and he began to just kind of open up his life and share about challenges he was facing and asked me to pray for him and stuff like that. Sometimes he and I would go out to lunch together, and other times Billy would go and maybe Paul Pankey or even Dee Powell. But for the most part just he and I would go and just sit and chat. As I think back on the number of times that he gave to the school, I never asked him, never asked for any money. God was really moving on his heart to do it. As we were going into the summer, we had another need and I never said anything to him. He said, "Well, I have another gift I want to give to you." I almost ran off the road when he told me how much it was. I think it was another $100,000, and that really carried us through the summer. Man, you talk about the pressure off me. Of course then the second floor was built and by that time, Carl and I were in grad school and so we already left and went up to Covenant.

TY: **...and the big check came around that time?**

RON: That was a total surprise. I was at home one day and Billy called and had Bill on the other line, a three-way call, and he said, "Guess what, I've got good news!" We chit-chatted and a few minutes into the conversation he said, "You know, I've been doing some thinking and you know what, that school is hopeless, (laughs) you guys are hopeless over there at that school." And I said "You know what, you're absolutely right, we are. We realize that we are hopeless without God." He laughed and said, "Yeah, that's what I meant." He said, "Well, when I come back, I want to meet with you guys." So the following week when he got back in town, me, Billy, and Dee Powell met with him and we went to his favorite place, which was Ruth's Chris... (laughter). I enjoyed that ride; it was good eating and good conversation. We talked about a whole lot of things and we finally got down to business and he said, "Hey look, my wife and I have been talking and we've made a decision and we want to give the school a million dollar gift to help set up an endowment." Of course we were all eating and forks stopped in mid-stream and we kind of looked at each other. When I looked up at him, he reached into his coat pocket and pulled out a blank check and hand-wrote out a million dollar check and reached across the table and handed it to me. Of course we were all speechless at that point. It was very affirming to me as an African-American young man to be receiving a million dollar check from a white man - the fact that he didn't hand it to Bill, he didn't hand it to Dee. So even as a symbolic act, he was saying, "I trust you." That meant a lot for me - because he could have just handed it to Billy. He was the board chairman, but I think he was trying to communicate something in that to me: "That I trust you and I affirm you in what you are doing." That was a signif- icant moment for me just in my growth as a leader and in a lot of ways even in racial relations because you know, it's like: *you don't think a white man is going to give a black man a million dollars, are you kidding*? But here again, it was a situation where we didn't ask for the money, it was just God moving on his heart and so that was a significant moment.

TY: **I guess in closing, is there anything else in terms of Restoration Academy and the impact it's had, not just on you but on the community?**

RON: Restoration Academy has made its mark on a lot of people's lives, the least of which being my own. But it has touched a lot of folk and I think it's still one of the best kept secrets here in the city. It's kind of flown under the radar screen for so many years. It's never been a powerhouse type school in a lot of ways. It didn't have these powerful boards, it didn't have a lot of things going for it, that you would think of when you hear about a school. But one of the things I think that it had that set it apart, it had the presence of God there. God ordained it and God sustained it and it kept us all on our knees before God, seeking Him. I think a lot of us who are connected with it have always felt this sense that God kept strengthening our faith, expanding us and helping us trust Him in the midst of it, and it was a great ride. Don't get me wrong, I wouldn't go back and change anything about it. I wouldn't change the times I had to sit in those triage sessions. I wouldn't change not getting paid early myself because of what God worked in me as I know He did a whole lot of other people's lives. From parents and students, to the teachers, the board members, every body's lives were touched. God used that school to touch the lives of so many people in so many different ways.

I think the one constant thing was teaching folks how to trust Him. We all came from different backgrounds, a lot of the board members had financial means, but that was no match for the needs that Restoration Academy had. So when you think about some of these guys that had some means, it was insurmountable compared to what they were able to do and so all we could do was depend on God. We didn't have these real huge financial backers and things like that. So, I'm pleased at where it is and where it's going to go. I just think that nothing but good things are going to continue to come from the school as it stays the course and remembers it's roots, not losing sight of where it came from, and how it got where it is. And maintaining that spirit that is true Restoration. But I think it's grown up. The school needed to make some changes and I think it's moved in the right direction. It is a school, but it still has that ministry focus to it that is about nurturing and caring for kids. So I'm excited. I felt good when I left, I feel good about it now and I sleep good at night. I don't

bite my nails and worry over Restoration
Academy. It's in a good place.

CHAPTER 8

"They Do Discipline" with Ms. "Cookie" Griffin

BIOGRAPHICAL SKETCH: *Cookie Griffin has been a part of the Restoration Academy family for five years. She came to the school in 2003 with four of her sons. She has taken six boys into her home through adoption and as a foster parent. After four years of working with the school as a parent she came on board as an employee. She now serves as the receptionist at the high school campus. Today she manages the office and she helps counsel a lot of the high school girls who come to her for advice and encouragement. She resides with her six boys and her daughter in Ensley.*

BEN: You've been at the school now for about four or five years and I'd love to hear a little bit about how you first heard about Restoration Academy and what first drew you in to taking your boys to the school.

COOKIE: I first heard about Restoration Academy through Ms. Armstrong. She had a son

143

that went here, Josh Armstrong. My boys were in the public school. They used to go to a small public school, the school closed down and they annexed them to a larger public school. Once they got there, they just literally shipped out. They said they wouldn't do nothing, they just literally shipped out. I said, "This is not going to work. I have to find somewhere for my boys to go." So I came and got an application for Restoration Academy. The first day I met Mr. Sciacca, I just sat in his office and cried, because I just wanted my boys to get in here and I'm so glad they came out here. I have seen a 180 degree turn around in my children, especially Steven. It is just amazing how Steve has changed, I mean, the spiritual leadership, the male role models, it's just amazing. Sometimes I just feel like I'm a PR person for Restoration because everybody I see that has kids, I'm talking about the school. I brag on Restoration.

It's overwhelming when you walk through the doors at Restoration, how you can feel the love. Everybody is just like one big family. If you're hurting, they come to your rescue. I just can't put into words how I feel. It's just a great feeling to be around so many Christian people and you see the reflection of the kids. Another thing good about Restoration is what you instill at home, the school passes on down to the child. So the kid is getting it both at home and from the school, and that's great. You've got to be careful what you do because you never know who's watching you, and I have been out in public, and I get so many compliments about the way my kids act and how respectful they are. Even so, I have had people, since I've been working at Restoration, that come off the street and ask about Restoration because they noticed the kids walking up and down the alley and they talk about how quiet they are, how they're not loud and running and saying other things. You know, they're just praising. I got the opportunity to work at Restoration because I had gotten laid off my job. One day I was talking to a teacher and I said, "You know, I'd like to work for Restoration." The following week, I got a call to come and work for Restoration Academy so it's just been a blessing. It's just a blessing to be around so many Christian people. I mean, you just don't know how I feel... it's a good feeling.

BEN:

Several of the boys in your home are adopted or foster kids, and you mentioned about the male role models at the school... is there any background information that you would feel comfortable sharing about the boys... how Restoration is meeting their needs or helping them based on where they've come from?

COOKIE: Yes, I have four adopted and two foster and as usual, most of them are in foster care or came to foster care because of drugs. Both parents or either parent was on drugs. I'm a single parent and I have no older brothers, so there's no one in the family they can look up to. But by them being at Restoration, most of the teachers at the high school are male and it's just great to have them around male Christian teachers. They do a lot of things for the kids, camping trips and just showing them the right way. I mean, anyone can go out there and drop the pass, but show them the right way to go. Right now there's so much peer pressure and stuff going on with these kids...well I might as well tell you, in the black community. It's just so hard for a child to grow up now. It is so hard. It's not like when I came up where everybody in the neighborhood chastised you for what you did and you got a whuppin' from them and then when you got home you got another whuppin'. But now the parents are just altogether different. It's even different with my child. My daughter is twenty-nine and things have changed from when she came to school until when my boys went. It's just a totally different world and it's nice to have something like the old schools come back into play, like at Restoration, you find that here and I love it to death.

BEN: **Do any of the boys have a relationship with their dad? Have they seen them?**

COOKIE: No. I have six boys at the house. None of them. I know all of my boys. I know they have mothers and I try to instill in them to keep in contact with their parents because they still should know who their parents are, and I try to keep them going and so far it's been working.

BEN: **Most of your boys play sports, any benefits that you've seen from the sports programs or any of the coaching staff?**

COOKIE: I have, I have. Mr. Coker has been wonderful. He is just like a dad, and Coach Pritchett. They're just like fathers to my boys. I tell Mr. Coker all the time, "I'm so glad my boys are around you, you are great." Which he is. He spends a lot of time with the boys at Restoration, and so does Coach Pritchett. They really are great people, great people.

BEN: **You said you kind of do some PR for the school. If there was somebody you were trying to recruit, what are the main things you would tell them?**

COOKIE: First of all, I tell them that Restoration is a great school. You don't have to worry about all the metal detectors, and also you don't see police around this school.

But one thing about it, I'm going to tell you right now, if you don't want your kids to be spanked, don't bring them up here because **they do discipline**. Most people say, "Oh that's OK. That's what they need." But I tell them it's a great school and I tell them, if they don't do their homework, they are going to do it regardless because ten weeks down the line, they are going to see that they still do their homework. That's incentive to get it done because if it goes undone they're going to get an "F" and they're still going to have to do it. They might as well go and do the work and get a grade for it then do it later and not get a grade. That's what I like about it.

BEN: **Talk about your job. I know this is your first year, but talk about your job in the office. For a while obviously you were an involved parent, but now you get to be not only an involved parent but also an involved staff member. How have you enjoyed the role, being in the kids' lives, what have you enjoyed about the job and the opportunities it provided you?**

COOKIE: I like it. I'm a people person, I like being around people. And I just noticed, I guess there's just something about me where the kid's just come to me. A lot of the girls come in and want to sit down and talk about things. What's going on at home and I try to tell them the right way. What to do, I tell them, you got to sit down and listen. You can't just jump and run your mouth, you've got to listen. You're still a child. I have no problem with kids, even the boys. They're good kids. They are.

CHAPTER 9

"Finally the Lightbulb Came On" with Eugene Law

B IOGRAPHICAL SKETCH: *Eugene Law came to Restoration Academy in 2002 as a seventh grader. He witnessed the school when all the students in grades K4 through 12 were compacted in what is currently the elementary building. He was one of the key players to help resurrect the Bulldogs 8-man football team after the school was without a team for almost five years. During that time, he won three state championships and one national football championship in 8-man football. He was also a key player in two state championships in basketball. In addition, he was the first student in Restoration Academy history to take a Calculus course. He graduated in 2008 and is currently a freshman at the University of Alabama. Of approximately 500 incoming freshman, Eugene scored number one on the mathematics entrance exam in Calculus.*

BEN: You've been at the school for six years now. You graduated. When you look back at the six years as a whole, what are some of the things that stick out in your memory the most?

EUGENE: The reading program and the math program. Before I came to this school, my other school didn't really emphasize reading as much as Restoration does. When I came here and saw how many books we had to read in English and History, I thought I wasn't going to be able to make it. But it's such a good school. They give you the one-on-one time - and they help you. The small groups in reading help you understand the books, so I ended up enjoying the reading program. In the math program, the teachers give math homework on the weekends. You get quizzed on it right after you finish your homework. It just helps you learn your work a little bit more, and encourages you to put a little more time into it.

BEN: Talk about some of the teachers you had over the years. Are there any teachers you had that stand out? Or anything you felt that was different about them as opposed to teachers you may have had at other schools?

EUGENE: Yeah, Ms. Edwards, she spends time teaching you the lesson and she gives you help when you need it. My other teachers, at other schools, they just get up at the board and tell you this is what you have got to learn for this test and they don't hardly put any work into it to show you how to work a problem. But Ms. Edwards, she is right there. When you take the quiz, she's taking the quiz right by you, doing the work. It's not like she's just looking at the answer key and marking off the answer sheet. She's doing the work too, so I think that's real good. The teacher's doing the same work as the student.

BEN: **Any other teachers that made an impact on you? Maybe academically or otherwise? Character or life skills or anything else that sticks with you that you learned at the school?**

EUGENE: Mr. Coker, when he was my homeroom teacher in the seventh grade. He taught me a lot. He taught me how to stick with it. Like during our first year of football, I remember quitting the team and when I came back, it wasn't like he came down on me or anything. He just welcomed me back in and taught me how to press through hard times. Even though we had a terrible season, he just told me it's going to get better and it did. We ended up winning games before I knew it, so it was good.

BEN: **You played basketball and football half of your time at the school. For the first few years you were there, we didn't have much of anything other than**

basketball. **How do you think sports helped shape for you where you are going in life right now? Do you see any benefit to you? And if so, how do you think sports helped you as a student and as a young man?**

EUGENE: Sports helped me to get through my work. Even though I knew sometimes, like in basketball we would face giants, teams that we would think were unbeatable. It also helped me look at my work like I'm coming up against this big test - this giant test - that I'm about to take. I was able to do it on the football field; I can do it in the classroom also. It pressed me to do my work in the class, too. I did this hard problem in class, why can't I go out here and tackle this 300-pound lineman or something.

BEN: **If some kid your age was looking for a school what would be one or two things you would tell them about why they should go to the school, something that a young person might be excited about?**

EUGENE: First, I would tell them about the good one-on-one time the teacher has with the students. I'd tell them about the sports. It's just like being in the classroom, but you're playing ball and they take that serious too and make you give it your all. And just the good friends you make with the teachers, but you still have them as a teacher; you still respect them as your teacher. It's just like they are real cool with you and you get to share with them your experiences; like how you're feeling inside your house. And even with the spiritual relationship, you get to share your heart with them and you know that they won't go out, spilling it out there to the world without your permission.

BEN: **Touch on the spiritual a little bit more. We talked about Restoration Academy academics and sports. Spiritually, do you think you grew during your time there?**

EUGENE: Oh yeah. I feel like I did spiritually grow at the school. First, I was kind of shy about talking about God but as I went from the seventh to the eighth, through the 12th grade I saw how the teachers... they shared their experiences, how they were in the same shape I was in - they had felt like it was un-cool - but how they found that there are some cool Christians out there in the world. They sent us out to meet people - like small groups, luncheons and stuff. So I really grew through that and now I'm able to share my belief with others.

BEN: **When you look back and think about friendships, peer culture at Restoration Academy...any memories that stick**

out? Being there as long as you were, is there anything about the kids, the people, relationships you had, that was different from your experiences in other places?

EUGENE: Well it wasn't quite different because how I saw it was, you just have to pick your friends out right because there are always some bad people out there in the world that think it's all fun and games. You have to surround yourself with good people, good Christian people that want to do the same thing you want to achieve in your life. I saw a lot of friends I had at the school get put out of the school cause they made the wrong choice. And I know giving up on them wasn't Restoration's fault - they accumulated all of it. They were doing the wrong thing every time you looked around. So I just kept my friends wisely and they had the same goal I wanted to achieve.

BEN: **As you distance yourself from Restoration, is there anything from the school you think you will take with you the rest of your life?**

EUGENE: I remember the moments I had with my teachers and the sports memories, but especially the teachers. Even though sports is real big with me, I'm going to remember the relationships I made with my teachers. That's real big to me because most of the time, teachers don't even want to spend any time with you outside of school, they'd be like "Hey, it's time to get out, go home." (laughs) But I made real cool relationships with my teachers. They'd invite me over to go do some things with them, go down to the lake house...

BEN: **Take you snipe hunting...**

EUGENE: Yeah... (laughs) It's been real cool. I love playing ball, love playing ball... but the teachers... you ain't gonna be able to find nothing else like that.

BEN: **Anything else on your heart?**

EUGENE: Yeah, I just remember how I don't know how I made it out of elementary school at a public school. I just made it through; I don't remember doing any kind of work. I don't remember taking any kind of tests, quizzes, homework assignments, none of that. But when I made it to Restoration... I just thank God that I did make it out of the public schools with at least a 'C' because I just don't remember any kind of work. **Finally the light bulb came on** when I started coming to Restoration and I just started getting my work done. Some people say I was already smart when I got there, but I think the light bulb just turned on by being in such a good environment. It related back to my household because I think I felt the same spirit that I felt from my house being right there at the school with me. So I was comfortable being there. It was just home, just feeling at home. Just a real good feeling to have because other schools, I knew I'd have to fight every day. Every day I would have to fight somebody. Even though it doesn't seem like that's the type of person I am, that's all I remember. I would pass by fighting... kindergarten, first grade, second grade, third grade ... all the way through just by fighting. That's the only thing I remember. I don't remember getting out any kind of work. No tests, quizzes, none of that. At Restoration, they just took their time with me, showed me how to take notes... basically once I got it down pat, I was like "I'm going to take over this school, win student of the year and all that." I just spoke it up, achieved my goals.

BEN: **Now you're off to Alabama, going to be an accountant so you can come back later with a big check for the school...**

EUGENE: Yeah (laughs)

CHAPTER 10

"That's Where
I Got My Attitude"
with Lesley Gooden

B IOGRAPHICAL SKETCH: *Lesley Gooden came to Restoration in 2002 as a sophomore. Lesley was a solid student during her three years at Restoration Academy and graduated with a strong academic transcript. She left behind a legacy of hard work. She and her mother were advocates for the school throughout their time there. They both used to volunteer at Restoration Academy events to share about their experiences at the school. Lesley went to the University of Montevallo for a period of time and is currently enrolled at Virginia College and working on her degree to be a Paralegal.*

BEN: One of the things I'd love to know about
                    is what was your first reaction when
                    you came to Restoration Academy? I
                    guess you came as a sophomore, what
                    were some of your first reactions when
                    you came to the school?

LESLEY: My first reaction was probably that it was a small (school), but I came from a small school with a very mixed history so I was very interested in what was going to be different. I actually started kind of in the summer so I was kind of like: "Ok, this is different." But once I got here and got to know people, I really got that "this is just a big family" feeling. That was probably my biggest thing throughout all of my time at Restoration is that it was a big family. That was my first impression. Wow, OK, everyone knows everyone. I'm not used to this. But I like it because I am very big on family and I enjoy knowing all those in my surroundings.

BEN: **You took some harder courses when you were at the school. Any specific classes that you really enjoyed and perhaps some that you had to dig in deep to pass or perform well in, that you look back on?**

LESLEY: Definitely my favorite class would have to be history. And I'm not just saying that because Mr. Sciacca's interviewing me. But my history classes challenged me and I got a chance to learn many new things. It was just one of those things that really fit my personality. Challenges? Math. I never liked math; I still don't like math. But Ms. Edwards really found a way to make me dig into it and really work hard. Toward the end we were kind of shaky, but she always found a way to help me to get over the dislike and get through the work, and learn what I needed to learn. And I think I wound up learning more life lessons in math than actual math lessons.

BEN: **Can you explain that, about the life lessons?**

LESLEY: I learned to stick to it and not to give up just because you don't like it. And that sometimes you have to do things that you don't like in order to become a better person. My math classes definitely made me a more determined person because they got me over my fear of failure. I think one of the first things I told you when I first saw my math grades was "I've never failed anything!" It taught me that it's OK to fall. The glory is not in falling. It's in getting back up, pushing through - even though you know that you may not be above average. It taught me that it's OK to be average, it's OK not to be great at everything; it's OK to have a weak spot.

BEN: **Over those three years, any specific memories or stories that stick out? What do you look back on?**

LESLEY: There are so many. Probably the time that I spent with the people who were in my classes. We were definitely the big mish-mash class. Everybody had something that they didn't like or something that was going on at home. But I think the one thing I will never forget about Restoration Academy was my junior year, when my dad died. Somebody called the school and whoever it was, I wish I knew so I could thank them, whoever it was told them what was going on. I will never forget when we were leaving the church and looking up and seeing just about all my teachers sitting as a group. And for those who weren't there, when I came back to school, just the warmest reception. I remember my first day back at school was really hard, and I remember looking down to the first floor by the office and I remember just bawling my eyes out. I cried and cried. Mr. Wright and Mr. Shepherd both came out and they were just so encouraging, and just that feeling of love that was given to me that day because it was just really a hard day, and just the love that was given to me that day is probably the one thing that I will remember all my life. It's just understanding, you know, how you can become so close to people. I actually felt like they felt what I was going through and that they wanted to be there and wanted to understand and wanted to help me over that. That was probably my most memorable moment at Restoration.

BEN: **When I look at you as a graduate, or any of our graduates really, you guys are what the school is all about.**

Students who have gone through the process and now are on the other side. If someone randomly stopped you at a grocery store or somewhere and said "Hey, you're a Restoration Academy graduate," and if they asked you a specific question on what do you think the school's primary mission is from your graduate perspective, what would you say you think the school's primary mission would be?

LESLEY: Oddly enough people have asked me that question and honestly, it sounds so cliché to a point but it's really bridging that gap between family, church and community. Because for so many kids that come here, from the situations that I remember... kids that came here came from broken homes, poverty level homes, and single-parent households. There was more of a loving understanding and a loving guidance towards where we needed to be. In addition to that, just the family environment, of course there's no way to substitute for a missing piece. It kind of helped you to see because so many of the people who worked here, their families were involved with everything. I remember Mr. Lynn's wife and all their kids, and you and your wife and all your kids and it just gave us that sense of a family. You were never so disconnected from anybody. You always had somebody to talk to. I think that's the one thing that Restoration has always done

- "what do you need, we're here for you, we're here to help you.' And it's always been about being a place that cares. It has always been about breaking the generational curses of family and preparing the students to be better than they ever could have imagined. It's about overcoming what society says about you and living according to what God has planned for you and desires you to be.

BEN: **The hope of this book is that it will be used ultimately to point to God's glory... for 20 years it's a long history for a small school. Is there anything else that you think needs to be in the book?**

LESLEY: Just that you are a wonderful bunch of people. It's funny when you go to Restoration, it's not always a positive thing while you are there. It's one of those things that you don't understand or appreciate until you get older. I did not gain an appreciation for things that I learned from Restoration until after I graduated - after I left college and actually in the midst of my divorce. That was really when I gained an appreciation and an understanding because I was able to look back on so many of the things that I was taught here. You know, the stick-to-it attitude. The "God's got a plan even though you don't understand the pain" attitude. It's something about it, no matter how far away you get, you always find those thoughts falling back into your head. It's so funny because I'll face things and it's like literally I'll have little reminders of people at Restoration - I can hear the different things that I was taught. I think that's probably one thing for me. No matter how far away I get, there's always a little piece of something that reminds me of Restoration.

I've had people who knew my mom, who ask for school recommendations, and the first place we say is Restoration Academy. It's one of those places that once you go, you can never forget. Regardless of how long you're here, it's a lasting influence. Even if you try to push it out of your mind, you can't. At this point, if I had kids, I would send them here. Because I know the quality of the people here. But like I said, you are not going to enjoy it as a student. That rarely ever happens. I know very few people who go here and say "Oh, I love it! I love it! I love it! I love it." But when you get older, it's when you hit those milestones in life that you remember, "That's where I learned it. **That's where I got my attitude**, my outlook." You remember the beginning. But it's hard to see the value of it while you're there. Looking back, I'm thankful for the time I spent here. I'm thankful for the arguments with teachers, the punishments, the hard things. Because the studying prepared me for the outside world. It taught me that nothing comes easy. You have to work for everything you want. And that's the thing: What you learn at Restoration is so much more than what's in the book, you learn life.

As with all places, it is not perfect by any means but when you leave, you leave with a better and clearer understanding of who you are and what your purpose is. You leave better than you come in and you know that you can make it through anything. You leave knowing that you are better. You leave ready to face and conquer the world. You leave finally understanding your place and purpose in the world. You leave with an understanding of who you are in God...

CHAPTER 11

"Learning to Loiter"
with Barbara Barker
and Mary Hargrove

B IOGRAPHICAL SKETCH: *Barbara Barker was approached by Carl Lynn in 2005 to help pioneer a prayer ministry for Restoration Academy. She accepted the request and rallied together some of the women from her bible studies to join her. After a few times down to the school, she and some of the others started to volunteer by reading to the children and tutoring. Before long Barbara and her friend Mary decided that a high school bible study for girls would be a better fit. For the last three years they have been leading a weekly bible study with high school girls and they have developed some amazing relationships. In addition, Barbara and several women from her bible studies have volunteered on a monthly basis to provide and serve lunch to the guests at Restoration's monthly visitors' luncheons.*

BEN: **What I want to ask both of you is how you first heard about Restoration Academy, and do recall some of the**

things you heard about the school at that time?

BARBARA: Because we were involved with Dr. Gordon's church. We were sort of involved with the work of the church. We were all just real interested in what was going on, not as intimately as we are now, but just praying for it and aware of it, but also trying to find financial resources to keep it going. And then for some reason it just stayed in my awareness - Restoration Academy, Restoration Academy. I knew we prayed for it at Briarwood and I knew a lot about it like that. But one day Carl Lynn just called me to come to see me, and it was interesting because I had been praying that God would show me a place beyond my borders where I could be used. And he just made an appointment. We sat in the ballet office, and of course I had known his grandmother so well... who was such a saint. He just told me out of the blue that God had put me on his heart to work on that prayer campaign for the building. I just couldn't believe that he had come right when I was praying. I said yes. We started our prayer groups, the people we knew, and we came out and did some prayer walking. We met up here at the school and I got them to print out the student body list so we could all divide up the names and be praying for the students. Then my daughter Peggy came out and did the musical thing, and she begged me to come with her, but I was teaching a Bible study at my home and then I just got to thinking, "No, these women have 50,000 opportunities for Bible study, I want to see if anybody wants to go with me out to Restoration Academy." And so we came. Carl likes to say we "hung out." I don't like that. (laughs)

BEN: **I think he used the word "loiter"**

BARBARA: Loiter. **We just loitered around.** Yeah. And I didn't like that. But Ms. Rose took me in and let me come in and teach the Bible study and then spend the rest of the morning in tutoring...which is not my gift. But I just fell in love with this place. I felt the Spirit of God here. What impressed me so much was seeing you young people, living in the midst of your own world when the good life was so available to you, as people call "the good life." Like your daddy (Fran) said how much it meant to him that you chose this, to come out here, and gave up living in the suburbs with your friends. And to say "No, God's called me right here." To look at you young people that came to plant your lives and invest them like that. It just really did so much for me. And then to hear how God was answering prayers, that always calls me - to see how God is working. Ever since then I just come out here and feel like the Spirit of God is at work. I can't really give you any more

history than that except it just... it was...
I know the Lord just said, "You can have a
part" although it seems so little compared
to... to come over here and then go back
to my own little secure world over there.
It just feels very inadequate. But we do a
lot of praying for these girls while we're
on the other side.

BEN: **Thank you.**

BARBARA: Ms. Mary, I didn't mean to preach the
sermon! (laughs)

MARY: I think that my first exposure to Restoration
was at Barbara and Frank's Thursday
night Bible class when Carl Lynn brought
some of the students out there and they
shared what Restoration meant to them.
You all had this beautiful brochure that
night that I received a copy of. I was just
so impressed with those young people.
I think it was probably the second year,
Barbara that you were out here that you
just kind of tossed out one Thursday
night, "Anybody that would like to volunteer out at Restoration, I will be going on
Thursday morning," or something like
that. I started praying about that and I
thought, you know, I spend a lot of my
time taking in and I really was praying
for an avenue to give out God's word
and I thought, I cannot think of a better
opportunity to give out what God has
been pouring in to me. So I came out with

Barbara and I just kinda hooked onto her and said, "I'm going to go to that Bible study that you teach and be a part of that." That's where I've been now. As she said, we receive so much personal satisfaction and joy from the least little glimmer of light getting through and hearing some of the feedback from the girls. We're learning a lot from them. Some days we just have to accept by faith that what we're giving out, God's doing something with it and some days God just abundantly shows us that He's doing things. So, it's a wonderful opportunity and we appreciate the privilege of being here.

BEN: **It's a privilege to have both of you here. And I wanted to touch on the girl's Bible study that you have been doing now for a couple of years. What are some of the challenges of that and what have been some of the joys and blessings... as you reflect?**

BARBARA: I think one of the challenges is — I've been really torn between building a doctrinal framework for the girls — but being experientially pertinent to them. Here again, it is so hard for me to look at these little girls and think that they have been exposed to what they've been exposed to. To the family lives, to the... I mean for one girl to sit there and say her cousin was killed when he tried to rob somebody and he shot him, and pray for her brothers in prison and all of those sorts of things. It's just so totally different. We want them to have the doctrine... and we need to find out what it is they're studying on the other days. Like this fall, we discussed condemnation and really let them see what sin really is, and then justification. Now we are in the period of sanctification. We've been saved by faith, what is the purpose of it. We started "Why was I called? Why am I here?" Some of the responses just thrill our hearts. But one girl really gave us reasons to wonder if she's really come to Christ. She really didn't seem to know. So that's kind of hard for us to discern: "Do they really know Him, or not?" Sometimes it's obvious. So what we want to do is really go back to the Bible. What does the Bible say? But then how does that relate? That's my passion, that they know the Bible and that they also know it in some systematic sense. We did topical things, last year, things like relationships. (Mary) has done a couple really good things on abstinence and moral purity...

MARY: But it's real hard to relate to where they're coming from when there's murders and jail time and just things...

BARBARA: Ann Modder went to take one young lady home. She'd taken her out to lunch last year and she took her home and her mama said for her to just drop her off and Ann said "I could not leave her there." There were men hanging out, and so she kept her with her until her mother came home. But she goes back to that every day. Ann said, "I could not do that." But to see these kids and see where they're coming from. Now I get frustrated. I want to see them more excited of the privilege, and I'm sure they are, they just don't go talk about it, about this incredible privilege that they have to be in a place where they're loved and protected and really taught. I'm sure they are. They were all talking about a graduate who was in college who said that after being at Restoration Academy, college was a snap? Who were they talking about?

BEN: **Oh, was it Eugene? ...**

BARBARA: Yeah

BEN: **...at Alabama.**

MARY: ... And hearing another young lady talk about her high school now in Montgomery that she's doing work a grade-level down from what she was doing at Restoration.

BARBARA: That's something really that they sound excited about ... "Look what we're getting at Restoration Academy compared to..." That turns me on too, to hear them appreciate what they have. A lack of gratitude is just the most common problem in our

173

society. I think, according to Romans 1, it's one of the main places we broke off from God.

MARY:
So we get all excited when they say, "Thank you for the sucker." (laughs)

BARBARA:
(laughs) Yeah…. But just to see those things of understanding what a privilege they have. And listening to Talethia talk about how much she wanted to come back to Restoration Academy and how they wanted to come back so badly - as opposed to last year with two girls. We ended up with just the two of them one day when y'all went somewhere and listening to that anger and I mean it broke our hearts… but they came to our house for dinner! I was really surprised, after they told us how they hated everything and hated everybody and everything… and yet they came to the dinner and that was sort of encouraging. You know, we still pray for them, we are just fixed in on that. That even what seems to bounce off right now really will have tentacles that get fixed in them. But I can't imagine the heartbreak you all have. When you see somebody have to get kicked out. That just…. (pause)… but it's necessary, it's necessary… I just could never be in your… I'd always say "Oh well, it's all right, you come back." (laughs)

MARY: One of the things that makes this school quality is that you have rules and they have to be obeyed. It's just good training.

BARBARA: It's necessary!

BEN: That's kind of the culture of discipline that we try to, by God's grace try to maintain and instill...it's an essential ingredient, it really is.

MARY: It's just you have to be so brave to enforce it.

BEN: Well you know when James says not many of you should be teachers, I've wondered if maybe fewer should be administrators. (laughs) It is a tough...

BARBARA: I taught one year at Mountain Brook Junior High, the first year it opened, the ninth grade. I would give the football team detention hall or something like that for something and they would come to me and say, "Aw, Ms. Brown, if we have to stay in detention and don't go to practice, we can't play in the game this week!" And I'd say "Well... well OK, now you promise you won't do this again." And I'd let them loose every time. I had absolutely no control. (laughs)

BEN: Those are the tough calls. But we do that... by God's grace... that's all you can bank on.

BARBARA: That's right.

BEN: Well you guys have been faithfully doing this for a while now and you both are real busy ladies that have a lot going on outside obviously. What is it about the Bible study and even the luncheons and the ministry that brings you back?

BARBARA: The thrill to think we can have a part in it. I mean it's an awesome and humbling thing to think we have some little thing we can contribute, you know. In fact, I've said if anything ever happens to Frank, I think I want to come out here and get an apartment and live by the school. I want to have a ballet group out here. The school is such a big cumbersome thing right now with with five-hundred students and all the performances that I can't just walk off and leave it but that would be...

MARY: And it is a joy to be in this room where we were just serving drinks with the Jason's box lunches or something to five to ten people, and then to see what it has developed into, with fifty, sixty, seventy people being served. We just pray for God to bring people that want to be involved and He certainly has done that.[4]

BARBARA: I'm real passionate about getting people to see what's going on out here. I said if they could just come and see... that they would want to be involved too. I've had so many people say that. I'm real thrilled to have Molly (Stone) because I think one of our challenges has been to utilize volunteers well. Because when they want to come, how do you do it? Because sometimes they are more awkward than they are helpful and I know that's a real problem. I think that's a real special place to know how to use people so they get that thrill, "I'm one but... what is that way of saying... 'I'm only one but I *am* one.'"

MARY: "If not me, who? If not now, when?"...

BARBARA: Yeah, that sort of thing. Because I feel like a lot of people really want to find a niche where they can have some kind of a part.

MARY: And Carl's presentation is so first rate. It's just...

BARBARA: And as many times as we've heard it, I get thrilled every time I think about it. And again, I listen to Carol Payne talk about Bill Payne and how he loves this. And I think about what he laid aside, you know, to come. But oh, he would not be torn away from this place.

BEN: **Yeah, it's hard to get him out the door at the end of the day (laughs). He's faithful.**

...Well, I know you all are probably still in the process of figuring it all out, as we all are, in a journey. But if there were other people that you were perhaps talking to that had an interest in volunteering — something like you are doing, faithfully each week doing something like a Bible study. What are two or three things you think you might tell them, things you've maybe learned by experience, maybe warnings but also just some encouragements that you would recommend to them if they were coming into this for the first time?

MARY: Well I think just to hang in there and maybe if the first situation that you are put in, you don't seem to click with it, to just say so. Speak up and just find another avenue, a place to be plugged in and just keep at it long enough to really know if this is where God would have you be. And if you have that peace to know that this is where He would have you be, then be faithful no matter what. Barbara said one time just... I don't even know what we were talking about but it stuck with me, "Be there, wherever you are, be there, all of you instead of thinking about what I'm going to do two hours from now. If you're here for an hour, three hours, whatever, all of you be involved with that situation right now."

BARBARA: Wherever you are, be all there.

MARY: That condensed it. (laughs) I got the general thought.

BARBARA: But you know, again, I think it comes back to real study of how to utilize people and when people find a specific place they fit. As Carl says, sometimes **you need to loiter around** until you find your place. (laughter) You know the first year when my job was prayer leader and we tried to just come out and walk around, just stand outside the classes and just pray for the kids in that class and nobody knew we were here... I think we got checked in right, we weren't just invading... but I just said anything, even like that, to stand here and just look at these children one by one and pray for God's hand to be working in their lives. I said, even the little things like that that nobody knows you're doing, God uses that. I don't know any place [more than here] that needs that supernatural work of God's Spirit to combat the forces of evil. And I just, again, my heart just breaks when I think of these beautiful children and what they've been exposed to or what they've come from or insecurity that they would wonder: "Who is my daddy? Who's that man?" I tell you that poem that...

MARY: … Shannon wrote?…

BARBARA: Well, that one too. But, oh, what was his name?… "I wonder"

BEN: **Jerime.**

BARBARA: Yes, Jerime… "My son will never wonder who his father is." I read that all the time and of course the one Christian Edwards wrote that got Briarwood on it's feet and they couldn't sit down. They stood up and wouldn't quit clapping because it was so powerful. But the one that breaks my heart, and I can imagine, is Shannon. She has so much to give and that poem she wrote three years ago about neither black nor white...it was profound. I wanted to have it printed in the newspaper. And to think with the family situation like that and Beth (Braddock) told me about the house they lived in. But she could come and just look so pretty. Now, those are the things that could just do me in. I mean *that* does me in with the little contact I had. But to think you pour your life in to some kids like that and the circumstances of their life just…

MARY: But the last chapter is not written in those lives.

BARBARA: Oh, I know. I know.

BEN: That's right and that's where you have to put your faith. We so often want to script things or believe that a certain amount of input will create a certain amount of output in that child as well, but it just doesn't always work that way. Sometimes there's an immediate change and sometimes it is five, ten years down the road. As you have been a part of this, are there any ways you've seen it increasing your faith or perhaps just being a blessing to your own spiritual walk or yourself personally?

MARY: Well I know, just realizing as we pray for them during the week and some of the things they write down on their prayer requests. (pause) It's just, it makes God's grace for my own life overwhelming. But for His grace, there go I. And what they have to live with and in... and just asking God to make them generational bondage breakers in their own homes. Trying to get the truth of God's word on the level that they can receive it, realizing what they are living in daily is a challenge and...

BARBARA: One girl (reading her prayer card) says "Pray that my family would remain close with all of the things that have been happening." I don't know what those things are. And then they write, "Pray that I would make the best decisions for school after I graduate." And "Just pray for me not to be stressed, because it really

181

puts pressure on me." And we constantly pray for that grace.

MARY: …and for jobs. A lot of them have parents that aren't working.

BARBARA: …and "that I keep my head high and smile because some things can really get me down." And "relationships." I mean, the things they ask us to pray for are really precious.

MARY: We tried to get them to give us specific things to pray about for the people they mentioned.

BARBARA: We specially wanted them to tell us how we could pray for them - for their personal walk with the Lord, their family, whatever. Because we just couldn't pray for everybody in the world that they knew. We wanted to focus on them. Sometimes those prayer needs… like one girl just wrote on hers last week: "Pray for my family. My cousin got shot … pray for my brothers in prison."

So we, I can't tell you that we saw this child go from this point to this point specifically. We have seen some gradual changes and some feelings that we are in a place of being trusted now and you know, one of the ones that I had a part in scholar-shipping, I thought she was doing so well and then they tell me, (pause) she got pregnant. Which can happen to the finest little sweet Christian girls in the sweetest environment, the wrong moment, the wrong everything. So I know that doesn't mean her whole Christian life fell apart. But it just really hurts to see that because I thought she was doing well. But again, like you said and Carl says, we're in it for the long term. What God will do in the long term. That's one of the things about being older.

BEN: **What's the saying,..if you want to make God laugh just tell him your plans. There's some truth to that.**

BARBARA: But we really marvel at God's grace at providing for you all and providing this place and I want everybody in Birmingham to know about it.

APPENDICES

For centuries there has been great debate concerning the proper way to "do school." Discussions concerning pedagogy, curriculum, textbooks, and programs typically dominate. There is always wisdom in staying current on research as it relates to effective teaching methods or ways to increase student learning. Yet there is also a temptation to apply a cookie-cutter approach to education and simply replicate effective strategies or programs that are being utilized elsewhere. Jim Collins states in his book that "good is the enemy of great."[5] Simply making your school a good school can often be a temptation, particularly because we serve a great God who has called us to do everything great to His glory.

Restoration Academy has a very unique mission and therefore the school has worked prayerfully and diligently to establish a school culture that is dynamic, enriching, meaningful and efficacious to reach our particular students. To do so, the school has spent time researching other effective programs and finding ways to implement those programs into what the school is already doing. Yet at the same time, we believe that we are called to provide something incredibly different to meet many of the disparate needs of our student body. For instance, many of our students come from single-parent households and from poverty. They live in neighborhoods rife with crime and chaos. Such students have unique perspectives, needs, and struggles. The school has created five separate cultural distinctives to meet the various aspects and needs of each student. It would be presumptuous to insinuate that these five cultures are the *only* way to do urban Christian schooling, yet after twenty years of trial and error, research, and prayerful study of God's word, we believe that these five cultures are essential components for any urban Christian school to be truly effective in providing a holistic education to urban youth. This epilogue serves as a template for the five cultural distinctives that have made Restoration Academy the institution that it is today. Like most ministries that have been around for a long time, most of what we have learned we have learned from our mistakes. However, we trust and hope that anyone who is seeking to duplicate a similar mission can utilize this section of the book as a blueprint.

CULTURE OF INCARNATION

"And the Word became flesh and dwelt among us, and we have seen his glory, glory as of the only Son from the Father, full of grace and truth." -John 1:19, ESV.

Jesus left the splendor and peace of heaven to invade an ugly, violent, and chaotic world. He did this willingly. Instead of simply demanding that a fallen world learn how to figure it out, He left His home and gave up his life showing the world the way. He took on human flesh and invaded the world with the love, grace, and truth of heaven. What a beautiful reality!

Over the years, Restoration Academy has discovered that to truly minister to an urban community there must be an intentional thrust to put down roots in the indigenous community. Two-thirds of Restoration Academy's staff has either grown up in or relocated to the Fairfield community. Most of those who have relocated have families and children. They've moved because they feel called to engage the community on a whole different level. They don't want to merely call the children they teach "their students." They want to call them "neighbors." Such a step is called "incarnational ministry." Jesus incarnated this world (His place of ministry) with His physical body.

As stated earlier, this unique step is a "calling." It's possible not everyone who is called to urban ministry is called to live in an urban community, but we believe that it is certainly something that should be prayerfully considered by anyone who desires to get involved in an ongoing way. Believers will often pray about where to work and who to marry, and often the word "calling" is utilized in those types of conversations as well. However, calling is rarely discussed when it comes to where one chooses to live, particularly if one chooses to live in a stable and peaceful community. Yet, shouldn't we understand that where we live should always be a matter of calling, whether it's the suburbs or the Sudan?

Carl Lynn, the school's current Executive Director, often champions the virtues of the Virginia Pine. It is a seemingly plain and insignificant tree, but it plays a vital role in reforestation and environmental renewal. It takes root in places of erosion and decay and produces a flourishing forest. It is a resilient and determined tree that benefits the ecosystem around it and literally holds things together. God's people are called to be Virginia pines wherever they go. We are called to benefit our communities and to hold them together. Yet, anyone will be hard-pressed to find any communities in this nation that have been ravished more by erosion and decay than the urban communities.

Those staff members who live in the community view themselves as "urban missionaries." As one analyzes the life of Christ and His own incarnational ministry on earth one can see He suffered as we did and he experienced the woes we as humans experience (Hebrews 2:18). Part of living as an urban missionary entails experiencing the pains and woes of the community to which you minister. Gang activity and occasional drive-by shootings are no longer things you hear about on the evening news. At times they are activities going on just outside your living room window. When your students lament that their house was broken into or that the stereo in their car was stolen, you can relate because the same things have happened to you. The pain of the community becomes your pain because it's your community, too. The garbage in the streets is no longer something you have to drive by on your way to work; it's something you have to clean out of your yard each morning. Most urban communities have been painted in an unfair light. Too many movies and news segments have given the false notion that the streets are always full of violence and crime and that most residents dodge bullets on their way to retrieve the morning newspaper. These misrepresentations have caused many to fear even visiting urban communities. This is a tragedy, but with that said, there are different challenges in many urban communities that must be faced.

A culture of incarnation is established when God's people follow His call to humbly live as Virginia pines in communities that are eroding or have already eroded into hopelessness. These people seek to bring hope to the locals by getting to know their neighbors and their needs. They call the police when there's chaos in the streets, but sometimes they cross the street to engage in conversation those who are causing the chaos. These "pines" cut their grass and bag up litter because there is no quicker way to bring hope to the hopeless than to remove the demoralizing blemishes of trash and filth from the streets. People in struggling places gain hope when the question is no longer, "How can we help you with *your* problems?" but instead becomes, "How can we work together on *our* problems." Most people are looking for a way out of these areas of decay, it becomes a powerful statement of grace and love when others willingly decide to move in. Hope is contagious. Over time when God sends His agents of hope into an otherwise hopeless community, people start to believe again because they can see and experience the positive changes before their eyes. God's people are called and have the awesome opportunity to bring about this type of change. In the book, *The Tipping Point*, Malcolm Gladwell explains that if at least 5 percent of a communities inhabitants are high-status role models that the community will remain stable, but if the population of high-status role models dips below 5 percent, that high school drop-out rates and teenage pregnancy double.[6] This stat should give any believer great hope because it doesn't take much to flip a community. A few more Virginia pines in any community will do tremendous good!

189

As stated earlier, this process takes a great deal of time. It's a process that is often discouraging and sometimes even dangerous. The enemy, Satan, hates incarnational ministry and does everything in his power to eradicate Virginia pines from his places of erosion and decay. Many of our staff at the school have suffered for their choice to move into the community, but again these communities have been wracked by suffering for years, and so it is a misnomer to assume that we can move into a place of suffering and not experience it ourselves. Many staff members have had their cars and homes broken into. Two teachers were held up at gunpoint and one had a bullet crash through his porch window during a drive-by shooting. God is faithful and He has continued to protect and provide for everyone. Yet, we must remember that Christ willingly plunged into a world of suffering in order to reach people, and He died in the process. Suffering is a part of ministering to those who are suffering.

CULTURE OF DISCIPLINE (DISCIPLESHIP)

"A man without self-control is like a city broken into and left without walls." - Proverbs 25:28, ESV

Borrowing from the scriptural text above, the protective walls for young people today are increasingly being compromised and destroyed through a variety of enemies. The prevalence of television, unfiltered internet, and controversial music have emerged as powerful disciple-making entities in the lives of today's youth It has been estimated that televisions (including video games) are on in urban households around 76 hours per week. It is not much better in the suburbs at 56 hours per week. Much of the content in today's television, music, movies, and video games is rife with violence, licentiousness, and hedonistic glut. In his book, *The End of Education,* Neil Postman indicates that young people will have witnessed 500,000 commercials by the time they turn eighteen.[7] Commercials in and of themselves are powerful value-shaping mediums.

In addition, the dynamic and often rootless influence of our children's peer culture is equally persuasive. Kids are raising kids. Nearly 80 percent of eighth graders in this country go home to an unsupervised environment. The technology in their bedrooms and the children in their streets have become their new supervisors, mentors, and teachers. These divisive and controversial shepherds are scattering our young people in a variety of ways.

There is an old adage that "when the suburbs catch a cold, the city catches pneumonia." The symptoms brought about by living in unsupervised environments and environments that are saturated by the influence of anti-normative media are prevalent in both urban and suburban communities, but the effects are exponentially devastating in urban communities. Many of our urban youth have no walls left in their life when you consider that nearly 70 percent of them grow up fatherless and many of them dwell in communities wracked by poverty, violence, addiction and crime. In such an undisciplined (and in many respects lawless) environment our urban youth are growing up in a hostile and antagonistic surrounding with few places to hide and few entities to protect them. With an absence of true community, identity and a sense of belonging for many young men is found in gang affiliation.

Consider one young man who came to Restoration Academy in 2007. We discovered through his mentor that he was living at home with his single mom. One of his brothers was running the streets. He was forced to share a bedroom with his other brother, his brother's girlfriend, and their newborn baby. One can only imagine how he was expected to study in such a place. His situation is extreme but hardly peculiar. Or what can be said to a young lady after her drug-using mom tells her a few days after she graduates that her only way to establish herself in life is to get pregnant and to apply for section eight housing? This counsel was passed on to one of our young ladies not too long ago. Where are the walls of protection? Where is the godly advice, the encouragement, and the community structures where young people like these two can find and maintain hope? Where do any young people find hope and stability when they walk streets littered with trash and see the abandoned houses and the walls of the local businesses covered in gang graffiti? For most of these kids the answer is that there is no hope. It was this very reality that haunted Dr. Gordon and compelled him in faith to create an alternative.

I still remember one young man going through a gritty discipline situation at the school. With tears in his eyes he said, "I gotta make it here. I can't get put out. I gotta make it out of the ghetto." For many students who are familiar with the trauma and drama of the local school systems, they see that Restoration Academy offers a peaceful pasture where they can find hope and a future. Dr. Gordon founded the school to provide that type of peace and opportunity.

For the past twenty years Restoration Academy has existed to try and rebuild the walls for our students by providing them with a structured environment. As the Proverb mentions at the beginning of this section, a city without walls is akin to a man without self-control. Because of the chaotic environments many of our children come from, they have been raised to live chaotic lives. Some have never been required by their parents or their former schools to do their homework. Others have never been expected to follow through on a commitment, to meet a deadline, or to be punctual to an engagement. Still others have never received proper training on how to resolve a conflict, how to push through adversity, or how to deal with authority. For many children from stable homes and communities, these life skills are a normal part of proper home training. Yet for those who have not had such a luxury, these life skills are often foreign concepts and sometimes abrupt irritants to their normal way of life.

To help establish these walls of structure in a young person's life, Restoration Academy is passionately committed to a "culture of discipline." This component is a key and crucial ingredient to the success of the mission. To create this culture, there are several key aspects that must be addressed.

For one, rules and expectations that maintain the structure of a healthy learning environment must be effectively communicated and faithfully maintained. We preach a clear message at Restoration, "You can learn and behave or you can face the consequences of your refusal to do so." Simply put, in order to shepherd sheep there must be fences and there must be a staff and rod. Students at Restoration Academy learn very quickly they are expected to do their homework every night or they will face consequences. They must be in uniform each day with their shirts tucked in their pants. Students are required to be punctual to school each morning and be in each class on time. There is an understanding they must respect themselves, their peers, and their authorities. Disrespect, bullying, and mockery are never tolerated. The world primarily advocates a policy that if someone pushes you, you push them back, and if they curse you, you must be sure to get in the last word. Modeling the language of Christ in Matthew 5, we are committed to helping our students understand they are called to be "peacemakers," and retaliatory language and actions are not a part of keeping peace. This type of instruction is countercultural and entails faithful modeling by instructors and staff at the school in how they personally handle conflicts and tension that come their way each day. Yet, it also entails faithfully disciplining the students - in love.

Secondly, Restoration Academy is committed to allowing students to live out the consequences of their decisions. I once heard an administrator share that the current generation of students is being raised by parents who are more concerned about preparing the road for their children than they are preparing their children for the road. This is not just an urban problem. Too often parents have a desire to remove consequences from their children, particularly when their children make mistakes. Yet, in the real world when an employee consistently fails to show up to work on time or regularly turns in their work late, he or she is going to be fired without mercy. That's why at Restoration Academy every homework assignment is critical, and it's why the school puts a huge emphasis on punctuality. Again, we want our students to understand they will always be under authority whether it's their boss, a police officer, or simply the authority of the law itself. Arguing and rebelling against a boss or a police officer will result in real life consequences. That's why it's important for our students to learn the proper way to disagree with authority and how to humble themselves and obey even if they do not feel like it. It's for these reasons the school is uncompromising in its emphasis on disciplining students who rebel against their teachers, coaches, and parents.

Teachers and administrators at Restoration Academy are seen as shepherds. The students are the sheep and the student body is the flock. Scripture is full of shepherding language as it relates to raising, mentoring, and disciplining young people. The "good shepherd" in John 10 is someone who lays down his life for the sheep. He is one who knows all his sheep by name, and his voice is recognized by all the sheep. The good shepherd is relational. All of the shepherds at RA seek to establish dynamic relationships with the students. The relationships are predicated on trust, consistency, and leadership. There are obviously powerful sub-shepherds (or "hirelings" as John 10 indicates) in culture that are divisive and seek to lead the sheep astray and scatter them. It's for this reason discipline is such a key component to effective shepherding.

Some of the popular methods of discipline today espouse the tenets of behaviorism. Extrinsic rewards and consequences are used to modify behavior. Painful or uncomfortable consequences are used to compel a student to modify deviant behavior. Rewards and privileges are used to encourage a young person to pursue and display good behavior. These methods have been proven to improve classroom environments and alleviate some of the distractions and behavior that affect the learning environment. However; most of these methods do very little to address a young person's heart. There is nothing about this methodology that helps students understand sin, and there is nothing that aids them in intrinsically pursuing righteousness. A good shepherd addresses the heart because he loves his sheep. He wants them to understand he genuinely cares for them and he is leading them on paths of life.

As mentioned earlier, students live out the consequences of their decisions. If a student is disobedient, defiant, lazy, or tardy then he or she will receive a consequence. Like a good shepherd, the rod and staff are used to corral the sheep. This may include detentions, suspensions, corporal punishment, writing assignments etc. In the process of the consequences, the young person is engaged in discussion. He or she hears about the dilemma of sin in their heart. The student learns about the grace of Christ Jesus. The student receives insight from the teacher and from scripture on how he or she could handle the particular situation better next time. If there is restitution or reconciliation that needs to take place, the student is given steps on how to apologize or how to restore the relationship. This process is time consuming because the teacher or administrator must really engage the young person in conversation. Often times this is done after school or during a prep period. Even so, Restoration Academy believes this time is absolutely crucial to effectively disciple and shepherd young people.

One of the most significant steps Restoration Academy took years ago was expelling students from the school. Shepherding is a fragile and precarious task. Some sheep in the flock are often rebellious mockers who are unwilling to be shepherded. For several years there were classes that nearly became toxic because some of the students were committed to undermining the mission of the school, the authority of the teachers, and the discipline system that was in place. These particular students started to affect the rest of the flock and pull other sheep out of the fold. In most cases, these types of students were given many opportunities to deal with their issues, turn from their rebellion, and make the necessary changes, but there were some who were unwilling no matter how many conversations and interventions were implemented. Paul states in II Corinthians 7:10, "For godly grief produces a repentance that leads to salvation without regret, whereas worldly grief produces death." Godly sorrow leads to a changed heart and to changed behavior even if those changes are baby steps. Worldly sorrow is characterized by temporary and fleeting apologies or remorse that never engages the heart or a child's behavior. In the end it leads to death and destruction as Paul states. Therefore, students who are unwilling to make changes over a prolonged period of time are withdrawn from the school. This is obviously a heart-breaking but necessary decision Restoration Academy espouses to anyone doing significant ministry with young people. It is always a difficult decision that must be saturated in prayer, but at times the school must determine what is best for the whole flock, and at times this entails the dismissal of a sheep or two.

There is almost always a parenthesis put around a student and his situation before he is dismissed. The administration typically takes time to prayerfully consider the situation, the student, and the rest of the student body. A few years ago two students were involved in an on-campus situation that warranted an immediate expulsion according to the handbook. Both students were seniors and close to the finish line. Heartbroken, the administration expelled them after several days of prayer and reflection. The meetings with both students and their families were dynamic as the students were forced to face the consequences of their bad decision. But at the same time they heard a message of hope when they learned the school was willing to pay for tutoring and for their GED. The school told them geographically speaking they could no longer stay at the school, but they would still be a part of our prayers and hearts.

We must demythologize the notion we are any person's "last hope." For one, that is an arrogant and presumptuous notion. We are no one's last hope. Christ is everyone's last hope, and His loving hands are much broader than any institution or relationship we could establish. At times, we must also embrace the difficult truth that there are situations in which the most loving thing we can do for a young person is give them the desires of their error-laden heart. Jesus taught us this in Luke 15 with his provocative parable of the Prodigal Son. In that parable a rebellious son told his father he wanted his inheritance and he wanted release from his father's authority. In love, the father gave the son the desires of his heart knowing full well his son was about to embark on a journey of heartache and disappointment. This decision is a step of faith. Yet, the amazing thing about the father's love in this situation was he always left the porch light on and he waited with expectation for his son to come home. We know after the son had spent all of his inheritance on wild-living he found himself broke and friendless. To provide for himself, he hired himself to a farmer as a feeder of pigs. Starving and hopeless the young man found himself longing to eat the pig slop itself, and it's at this point the story takes a wonderful turn. It states that the young man "came to his senses," and longed for his father's embrace, his company, and his home again. The son returned and the father took him in again and lavished upon him all the love and affection in his heart. In similar fashion, we at Restoration Academy have taken the bold step of allowing perpetually rebellious students to pursue the desires of their heart with the hope and belief they will ultimately "come to their senses" once they recognize the path they have chosen is rife with disappointment. Sometimes eating with pigs is a more effective conduit of grace and truth than one more second chance.

Several years ago a young man at the school was expelled for some ongoing moral and character issues. Years after his dismissal, he returned to the school with his face all aglow. He told the administration God had used that expulsion to save his life. Outside of the school he hit rock bottom and then discovered Christ. He explained how he got active in youth ministry at his local YMCA and how God was using him to share the gospel in his own community.

The Culture of Self-Efficacy

It is no mystery that the United States is quickly falling to the bottom rungs of education in comparison to most of the industrialized nations in the world. Dropping test scores in reading, math, and the sciences have caused many educators to sound an alarm of concern. Recent research has shown that more than one-third of eighth graders in this country are reading below basic grade level.[8] Most students in urban communities are digressing by one-third of a grade level for every year they are in school starting in the third grade. This means a large portion of our students in urban communities are nearly functionally illiterate by the time they graduate from high school. In this country, it is very difficult to find a decent job if one is functionally illiterate. In fact, criminologists now are studying the percentiles of functionally illiterate youth in our nation to determine how many prisons must be built in the next ten years. There is a strong connection between functional illiteracy and incarceration because there are few economic options, besides a life of crime for someone who can't read. Recent studies have actually determined that eight out of ten of inmates are functionally illiterate.

Jesus instructed his followers to "clothe the naked" (Matthew 25:36). Dr. Gordon believed that the "naked" in an urban context were the functionally illiterate, and that Restoration Academy could serve as a ministry to provide clothing of literacy to urban youth. Many students who come to Restoration Academy in junior high and high school are well behind grade level in reading and mathematics. This lapse in learning is due to a variety of circumstances including but not limited to a failing public school system, lethargy on the part of the student, and a home-life that does not emphasize strong academic learning. Many struggling students have either been crippled or disillusioned by an environment that neither offers nor preaches excellence to them. The glorious truth is these students are not lost causes who have fallen through the cracks. They are gifted learners who need to be challenged. They are students who need to have their academic foundations strengthened so they can progress in building the future God has planned for them.

To meet the academic crises which are certainly most prevalent in our urban communities, Restoration Academy has sought first and foremost to establish itself as a "reading and math emphasis school." We believe reading and math are the gateway disciplines upon which the success of all other subjects is predicated. To help address our students' reading struggles we have utilized a reading program which was presented to our school by Briarwood Christian School. Nearly ninety a minutes a day, our students participate in language arts. Approximately an hour of that time is set aside to read and discuss novels. The students are taught several distinct critical thinking skills and visual tools to dissect, analyze, and comprehend the books they are reading. As they read their novels, they spend time implementing the skills and tools for each chapter. Then, they gather in small groups, discussing the nuances, themes, characters, and plot development of each chapter with their teacher. By the end of the school year, most of our students have read between eight and twelve novels cover to cover.

In an age saturated with technology including Sony PlayStations, the internet, and television, most students in this country are not avid readers. Yet, at Restoration Academy we have students asking if they can read their book during recess or inquiring whether or not they can borrow the book during the weekend. I can still remember one of our juniors, Fredice, saying with a big smile on his face as he waved his book in the air: "This is the first book I've read cover-to-cover in my whole life." Many of our students are falling in love with literature, but beyond that many of them are becoming proficient readers. In our annual SAT-10 tests, most of our students (particularly in the junior high and high school where the deficiencies are strongest) have jumped from two to five grade levels in one year in their reading comprehension. This is remarkable when you consider that statistics indicate most students in urban communities are digressing by a third of a grade level for every year they remain in school.

The reading program also considers readability. Too many reading programs offer students only one novel or reader per reading unit. Yet, this blanket approach does not work when in any given classroom you might have students who are a few grade levels behind in reading, those who are right at grade level, and a handful who are ahead. For each reading unit, each teacher distributes different novels to three different reading groups. That way a student can read a book that correlates to his or her level of reading comprehension. The goal is to provide a student with a book they can read and comprehend so they might "believe" that they can read and learn to love to read at the same time. For instance, if a struggling ninth grader received a copy of *Huckleberry Finn*, he would probably despair of hope by the second page and give up altogether. Yet, he might enjoy some threshold literature written on a fifth-grade level. Once he reads and digests a novel that he can comprehend he will be empowered with the belief he can read another book, even one that is more challenging. A child's belief that he or she can learn is called "self-efficacy." It is not dumbing down the literature or giving the student something that insults their intelligence. Nor is it just a simple boost to his self-esteem to help him feel better about himself. Self-efficacy occurs when a student accomplishes something that was challenging and yet doable. To provide a student with a novel that is both challenging and yet doable requires that the instructor knows his students and their challenges well. The program is very teacher intensive.

Restoration Academy seeks to provide students with self-efficacy in math as well. During the preliminary interviews, all students in grades six through twelve are tested in reading and math. Too often we find junior high and high school students who are well behind what the report cards from their previous schools indicate. For instance, we will often receive a sophomore in high school who received a passing grade in geometry from their former school, yet we discover through testing the student is still struggling with consumer math. Therefore, after testing our students during the initial interview process we place them in math courses that reflect their current comprehension. The goal is that in a short period of time we can help elevate them to a math course that is reflective of their actual grade level. To help concentrate on our math focus we have hired two full-time and one part-time math teacher in the junior high and high school.

Restoration Academy is not in the business of promoting students to courses they are actually ill-fitted to comprehend. This entails bolstering their mathematical foundation as mentioned earlier. To do this, our teachers provide rigorous environments and rigorous criteria for students to meet. In the junior high and high school, students attend mandatory math labs during the week to put in an extra hour one to two hours per week. Volunteers are brought into the elementary and high school to pull kids out of class and work with them one on one. We are convinced that we must exponentially provide students with extra time to get them caught up to where they are supposed to be.

Students also receive a healthy dose of homework in math each night as well. Mrs. Edwards, our upper-level high school math instructor, makes sure her students complete every problem on every assignment. If they skip the word problem at the end of the assignment, they receive a zero. It's not because they did not understand the problem it's because they didn't try. Any visitor to the school will witness students out of their desks and up at the white boards solving math problems or the students quietly working at their desks as teachers patrol the classroom, looking over the students' shoulders and providing instruction.

This culture of self-efficacy helps foster a belief in the students that they can achieve, yet it also helps establish a diligent work ethic. Because of the challenging environment, students must be attentive in class, faithful to their homework, and consistent with their attendance in order to pass classes. Students who rebel against or refuse to buy into the culture at the school typically struggle or fail altogether.

At Restoration Academy we believe it is essential for students to understand life grows increasingly more difficult. They must comprehend that they will have to work diligently, persevere against adversity, and think critically about the world around them if they want to grow and have success in the future. For many students in urban communities, there is a fog of despair and hopelessness in their lives, particularly as it relates to academics and achievement. We seek to dispel that fog by helping our students establish a primary foundation through proficiency in reading and mathematics. Secondly, we are determined to create a challenging environment in which students will be stretched yet empowered with the belief they can grow and have success in their life.

One mistake some schools make is buying into the temptation to try and address every academic need that arises with students. In an urban context, the needs are myriad. What can happen is a school can set up numerous programs to meet all of the various needs that surface, but the shortfall of such an approach is the school ends up bringing average results to multiple things instead of strong results to a few things. This concept is developed by Jim Collins in his book

Good to Great. He suggests that non-for-profits should ask one simple question: "What can we be the greatest in the world at?" The institution must highlight one to three things to which it can bring excellence. Collins calls these key things an institution's "hedgehog principle."[9] Restoration Academy's hedgehog principle in regards to academics is a relentless emphasis on reading comprehension and math. Bereft of strength in these two key subjects, students will struggle immensely, but once proficiency is established in these areas a student can flourish boundlessly.

CULTURE OF COMPASSION

"And your ancient ruins shall be rebuilt; you shall raise up the foundations of many generations; you shall be called the repairer of the breach, the restorer of streets to dwell in" -Isaiah 58:12, ESV.

The verse above is Restoration Academy's theme verse. It's a beautiful promise to God's people during a time of spiritual, socio-economic, and national crisis. With captivity looming for the Israelites, God made a remarkable promise to His people that at some point in the future they would be instruments of rebuilding the devastation, pain, and desolation in their own community.

We too desire that our young people become key stakeholders and instruments of compassion in their own ravaged communities and streets.

There is a problem today with American youth. This generation of young people is growing up with an increased sense of narcissism and entitlement. This is not an urban problem, but a national problem. Students increasingly are allowed and encouraged with their MySpace pages and iPods to create their own personal worlds to satisfy their own personal desires and interests. They are increasingly discovering it is possible to create a world around them in their own image. By perusing most young people's blogs and web pages you will find artwork, music and content that are incredibly myopic and self-centered. The prayer of Christ in Matthew 6 was that "God's kingdom would come" and that "His will would be done on earth as it is heaven." God's people are called to help refashion the earth in the image of heaven. Instead the world is being refashioned and perverted to reflect the image of man's wayward heart and passions.

In addition there are many well-meaning programs and institutions that are giving students too much. Most churches and Christian schools are committed to the well-being of the children within their walls. This is obvious. To maintain "well-being," many of these institutions have set out to provide cutting-edge technology, recreation centers, dynamic curriculum, climbing walls, exciting worship programs and other exciting venues to entertain the youth and also to provide them with the academic or spiritual tools they will need to be successful. Yet what often gets communicated to our young people through all these venues and programs is "it's all about them." Our young people end up getting spiritually, academically, and even recreationally supersaturated with the reality that life is all about them. This is a travesty when we consider that Jesus Christ desired that all of His followers would radically and consistently follow him by living a life outside of themselves that is spent on behalf of the needs of others.

To help counter and ultimately break this navel-gazing cycle, Restoration Academy is committed to helping our young people learn to live outside of themselves. This is not easily done. There is a false notion in some circles that the urban youth have nothing and that they are in need of everything. This is true in some respects when you compare their lives to those who are more economically privileged or perhaps to those who are a part of a better school system and neighborhood. But just like kids in the suburbs most youth in urban communities struggle with a notion of entitlement and self-focus. Entitlement and self-focus are universal battles that have been a part of the sinful fabric of mankind since Adam. So to counter these struggles, Restoration Academy has sought to put students in places of need within their community.

All students in grades K5 through 12th grade participate in quarterly Biblical Integration Projects (or BIPs). These are structured by the students' homeroom teacher and include a variety of focuses. The starting point is pursuing a project within the children's indigenous community. We want our young people to see themselves as agents of grace and change to their homes, streets, and neighborhood. Some of our students have adopted a quarterly aesthetic cleanup by scouring the streets and cleaning up litter. They have pulled weeds in a community garden and painted over gang graffiti along the backs of houses and businesses. Others have gone to the local half-way house and brought cards, songs, and food to the inhabitants. Some of our young people visit the local nursing home and bring joy and life to the elderly. One of our high school classes has gone to a nearby public elementary school to tutor their young students in reading. Our upperclassmen adopted a local man who is mute and deaf. He makes money cleaning up aluminum cans and taking them to the recycling plant. Our children collect cans for him and then invite him into the classroom to love him and encourage him. We have had others who visit one of the local homeless ministries to labor and bring food.

All of these opportunities are part of an ongoing attempt to help our students encounter people outside of themselves who have needs far greater than their own. When young people (or anyone for that matter) get an opportunity to participate in these types of encounters, several things take place. For one, young people gain a startling new perspective that there are others who have lives that are harder and needs that are greater than their own. They also realize that even though they're young people they can do something to improve someone's life even if it's a small gesture or an act of kindness. Thirdly, young people discover the mysterious joy that accompanies ministering to others. Joy always comes with following in the footsteps of Jesus and bringing water to the thirsty, food to the hungry, and visits to those who are locked up in loneliness and poverty. Christ found joy in His mission and He promised that others would experience that same thing if they followed Him.

At Restoration Academy, we also want our children to gain a heart for the world. By partnering with other churches and missions, we have been able to take some of our students on international mission trips to Peru and Guatemala. In the mountains of Peru, our students have participated in basketball camps. In the tiny town of Monjas, Guatemala, our students helped build a dormitory for orphan boys and provide a medical clinic to more than 4,000 impoverished men, women, and children. In these venues, our students looked abject poverty and hopelessness in the face and were given an opportunity to address it. Only 3 percent of missionaries from this country are African-American. We are committed to international missions and to allowing our children to bring the love of Jesus to every corner of the world.

Not everyone can go to Guatemala or Peru, so we have brought Guatemala and Peru to the classrooms. Every class supports a Compassion child. Pictures from children all around the world are posted on the walls along with their prayer requests and report cards. Our students send them monthly letters and pray for them on a daily.

We have discovered the mysterious power of compassion. True compassion exposes the false shroud of entitlement and snatches young people out of the snare of their own selfish hearts. It instills them with hope and purpose. Compassion exposes their hearts to the pain of the lost and hurting, while at the same time filling their hearts with the joy of seeing a lost and hurting individual receive hope and life.

Much of American culture (and sadly the American church) is committed to placing a glamorous mirror in the faces of our children so they are forever infatuated with their own reflection. A culture of compassion smashes that mirror with a sledgehammer and allows young people to instead see a dying and hurting world in the faces of their peers, the neighbor across the street, and in the eyes of the orphan across the ocean. After delivering bread to the starving and handing a bottle of medicine to the sick the iPod seems to lose its luster and the MySpace page becomes a shallow diversion. This culture of compassion is an essential ingredient to any legitimate ministry that seeks to expose children to the realities of following Jesus.

CULTURE OF ADVOCACY

"When the ear heard, it called me blessed, and when the eye saw it approved, because I delivered the poor who cried for help, and the fatherless who had none to help him. The blessing of him who was about to perish came upon me, and I caused the widow's heart to sing for joy. I put on righteousness, and it clothed me; my justice was like a robe and a turban. I was eyes to the blind and feet to the lame. I was a father to the needy, and I searched out the cause of him whom I did not know. I broke the fangs of the unrighteous and made him drop his prey from his teeth." - Job 29:11-17 ESV

The book of Job indicates that he was a "blameless" man. The passage above reveals why. Before the tragedies that befell Job, he was a man of means and a man on a mission. The verses above are Job's explanation of how he followed the generous heart of God by giving everything he had to the poor, the needy, and the hurting in his community. He even sought out the cause of those "whom he did not know." In the verses prior to these, Job explains how everyone in the community knew who he was and gave him an enormous amount of respect. Not because he was a man of great means but because he was a man who poured out his life on behalf of the disenfranchised. He was an advocate for anyone who had a need.

Restoration Academy has sought for twenty years to sound a trumpet on behalf of the poor in Birmingham. It is our belief that the purpose of para-church ministries like Restoration Academy is to call the Body of Christ to address the crises in our cities. For too long the issues facing our urban communities have been estranged from those who can help by miles of highway and a general indifference. But "issues" is not an adequate word. The greater truth is that the issues facing our urban communities are actually issues that involve real people with real stories. There are real children who are going to schools in hellish environments. There are real mothers who are struggling to keep the lights on and keep food in the fridge. There are real young men who are joining gangs because there is no other example of community on their block. The trumpet that the school is sounding is a call to all of God's people to plunge into the lives of our urban poor. An advocate is someone who somehow absorbs the pain, shame, and difficulties of another human being and makes that person and his or her issues a part of his life. An advocate is someone who bemoans the tragedies and strife facing so many urban communities and cries out that "enough is enough." An advocate states that the peace, comfort, and protection that he has provided for his own children and discovered in his own community is something he wants to provide to another child and to another community. Advocates give of their resources and their time just like Job.

Restoration Academy pursues advocates. To keep a quality Christian education affordable, the school must raise nearly $850,000 per year. This is a monstrous task, and yet God has faithfully kept this fledgling ministry in existence for twenty years. To Hm be the glory! There are a variety of ways to advocate at Restoration Academy.

Some seek to give up their treasure. For $4000 a year, a scholarship can be purchased for a student at Restoration Academy. This provides a young person with an opportunity to go to a school where he doesn't have to pass by police dogs and through metal detectors on his way to class. He doesn't have to concern himself with whether or not he's going to be jumped on his way home. If he's struggling with his math work he has a teacher who will stay until 6 pm to tutor him or he can just walk across the street to his math teacher's house. He finds out that when stuff gets dramatic and dangerous at his home, his football coach will take him in like a son. This young student experiences hope and love, and finds a place that can actually propel him forward in life and help him break generational cycles.

Other advocates donate their time. They show up and tutor struggling students. They mentor children through weekly Bible studies and individual counseling. Some come and read books and work on flash cards with elementary children. Others take children into their homes or take them to work and teach them about their jobs. There are others who help snatch our kids off of the streets by finding them jobs or hiring them themselves. Some take students on trips or to college ball games. They impart a message that they want to get to know the children. They want to hear their stories and learn about their families.

Still others pray for the school regularly. When they watch the news and hear about another shooting or crime in an urban community, they think of Restoration Academy and they pray for the school. They pray for the teachers, the administration, the students and the community. They also take hope that Restoration Academy is **addressing the urban crisis** in many ways.

The truth is God created and has sustained Restoration Academy to affect Fairfield with real hope and grace. But the teachers, staff, students, and families need the help of God's people to come alongside in a variety of ways. To truly affect the urban crises facing this nation it will take all of God's people to mount up as advocates and participate in bringing the beautiful message of the gospel to the streets. Our prayer is that God will raise up His Bride, the Church, to champion the lives of the urban poor and that She will bring the beautiful feet of the gospel to neighborhoods wracked by despair. We pray other visionaries and pioneers will hear this story and spark a Restoration Academy movement in their own hometown. The world will take notice when the dividing lines of race and socio-economics are abolished by God's people doing the work of Christ by following in His footsteps.

WANT TO BECOME AN ADVOCATE?

- **Come to a Visitor's Luncheon**. Restoration Academy hosts an informative luncheon from 12 until 1 PM during the first Thursday of each month (August through May). It's a great way to see what's going on at Restoration Academy and to witness what God is doing in Fairfield.

- **Provide a Scholarship**. For just $4000 you can provide a student with an opportunity to get a quality Christian education. This is a great way to bring real hope and opportunity to a young person's life.

- **Volunteer at the School**. There are host of ways to volunteer at the school. Volunteers can tutor, lead a small group Bible-study, speak in chapel, or simply mentor a young person in need. This is a great way to give of your time and to develop a powerful relationship with the students.

- **Support the Staff**. Sometimes it's easy to forget about the staff at the school. Most of them live in the community and they have specific needs at their home and in their families. There are many ways you can encourage the staff and help meet their needs.

- **Pray**. The ministry at Restoration Academy is in constant need of prayer. The teachers and students alike face many challenges, and there is no greater blessing than to surround the school in ongoing prayer for protection, provision, and peace.

If there are specific ways that you would like to become an Advocate at the school then contact the main office and ask to speak to someone in the Development Office:

Phone: 205.785.8805

Website: www.restorationacademy.org

Address: 4600 Carnegie Avenue Fairfield, AL. 35064

ENDNOTES

[1] At that time Jim Pinto was the rector of Christ Charismatic Episcopal Church in Fairfield. Today the church is Church of the Reconciler CEC.

[2] Mama Louis is the founder of Grace House in Fairfield which is a ministry to orphan girls.

[3] "Flowing music" was the type of music this woman needed so that she could prophesy. During the ceremony it took DeWayne Coker several tries on the piano before he could create the type of "flowing music" the woman needed.

[4] During the first Thursday of each month RA hosts a "Visitors Luncheon." Visitors get a chance to hear about the school, do a tour, and learn about ways they can partner with the Academy. Barbara and many women from her Bible studies have prepared food and served it at these luncheons for the past few years.

[5] Jim Collins. *Good to Great*. Harper Business: New York. 2001

[6] Malcolm Gladwell. *The Tipping Point*. Back Bay Books: New York. 2002

[7] Neil Postman. *The End of Education*. Vintage Books: New York. 1995.

[8] Jonathan Crane *The Epidemic Theory of Ghettos and Neighborhood Effects on Dropping Out and Teenage*

Childbearing. American Journal of Sociology (1989) vol. 95, no.5, pp 1226-1259.
[9] Jim Collins.

Printed in the United States
210657BV00002B/2/P

9 781607 911777